BOY SCOUTS OF AMERICA
MERIT BADGE SERIES

PLANT SCIENCE

"Enhancing our youths' competitive edge through merit badges"

Requirements

1. Make a drawing and identify five or more parts of a flowering plant. Tell what each part does.

2. Explain photosynthesis and tell why this process is important. Tell at least five ways that humans depend on plants.

3. Explain how honeybees and other pollinating insects are important to plant life.

4. Explain how water, light, air, temperature, and pests affect plants. Describe the nature and function of soil and explain its importance. Tell about the texture, structure, and composition of fertile soil. Tell how soil may be improved.

5. Tell how to propagate plants by seeds, roots, cuttings, tubers, and grafting. Grow a plant by ONE of these methods.

6. List by common name at least 10 native plants and 10 cultivated plants that grow near your home. List five invasive, nonnative plants in your area and tell how they may be harmful. Tell how the spread of invasive plants may be avoided or controlled in ways that are not damaging to humans, wildlife, and the environment.

7. Name and tell about careers in agronomy, horticulture, and botany. Write a paragraph about a career in one of these fields that interests you.

8. Choose ONE of the following options and complete each requirement:

35932
ISBN 978-0-8395-3396-2
©2014 Boy Scouts of America
2014 Printing

Agronomy Option

A. Describe how to prepare a seedbed.

B. Make and use a seed germination tester to test 50 seeds of four of the following plants: corn, cotton, alfalfa, soybeans, clover, wheat, rice, rye, barley. Determine the percentage of live seeds.

C. Tell about one important insect pest and one important disease that damage each of the following: corn, small grains, cotton. Collect and name five weeds that compete with crops in your locality. Tell how to control these weeds without harming people, wildlife, or useful insects.

D. On a map of the United States, identify the chief regions where corn, cotton, forage crops, small grain crops, and oil crops grow. Tell how climate and location of these regions make them leaders in the production of these crops.

E. Complete ONE of the following alternatives:

  1) Corn

   (a) Grow a plot of corn and have your plot inspected by your counselor. Record seed variety or experimental code number.

   (b) Tell about modern methods of commercial corn farming and the contributions that corn makes to today's food and fuel supply.

   (c) Tell about an insect that can damage corn, and explain how it affects corn production and how it is controlled.

  2) Cotton

   (a) Grow a plot of cotton and have your plot inspected by your counselor.

   (b) Tell about modern methods of commercial cotton farming, and about the uses of cotton fiber and seed and the economic value of this crop.

   (c) Tell about an insect that can damage cotton, and explain how it affects cotton production and how it is controlled.

3) Forage Crops
   (a) Collect, count, and label samples of each for display: perennial grasses, annual grasses, legumes, and broadleaf weeds. Indicate how each grass and legume is used. Keep a log of the site where you found each sample and share it with your counselor.
   (b) Explain how legumes can be used to enrich the soil and how they may deplete it under certain conditions. Explain how livestock may enrich or deplete the soil.
   (c) Name five poisonous plants that are dangerous to livestock, and tell the different ways of using forage crops as feed for livestock.

4) Small Grains
   (a) Give production figures for small grain crops listed in the U.S. Statistical Report or Agricultural Statistics Handbook for the latest year available.
   (b) Help in harvesting a crop of grain. Tell how to reduce harvesting losses and about modern methods of growing one small grain crop.
   (c) Visit a grain elevator, flour mill, cereal plant, feed or seed company. Talk with the operator. Take notes, and describe the processes used and tell your patrol, troop, or class about your visit.

5) Oil Crops
   (a) Grow a plot of soybeans and have your plot inspected by your counselor.
   (b) Modern methods of growing soybeans on a commercial scale, and discuss the contributions soybeans make to our food supply.
   (c) Explain why a killing frost just after emergence is critical for soybeans.

Horticulture Option

A. Visit one of the following places and tell what you learned about horticulture there: public garden, arboretum, retail nursery, wholesale nursery, production greenhouse, or conservatory greenhouse.

B. Explain the following terms: hardiness zone, shade tolerance, pH, moisture requirement, native habitat, texture, cultivar, ultimate size, disease resistance, habit, evergreen, deciduous, annual, perennial. Find out what hardiness zone you live in and list 10 landscape plants you like that are suitable for your climate, giving the common name and scientific name for each.

C. Do ONE of the following:

1) Explain the difference between vegetative and sexual propagation methods, and tell some horticultural advantages of each. Grow a plant from a stem or root cutting or graft.

2) Transplant 12 seedlings or rooted cuttings to larger containers and grow them for at least one month.

3) Demonstrate good pruning techniques and tell why pruning is important.

4) After obtaining permission, plant a tree or shrub properly in an appropriate site.

D. Do EACH of the following:

1) Explain the importance of good landscape design and selection of plants that are suitable for particular sites and conditions.

2) Tell why it is important to know how big a plant will grow.

3) Tell why slower-growing landscape plants are sometimes a better choice than faster-growing varieties.

E. Choose ONE of the following alternatives and complete EACH of the requirements:

1) Bedding Plants

   (a) Grow bedding plants appropriate for your area in pots or flats from seed or cuttings in a manufactured soil mix. Explain why you chose the mix and tell what is in it.

   (b) Transplant plants to a bed in the landscape and maintain the bed until the end of the growing season. Record your activities, observations, materials used, and costs.

   (c) Demonstrate mulching, fertilizing, watering, weeding, and deadheading, and tell how each practice helps your plants.

   (d) Tell some differences between gardening with annuals and perennials.

2) Fruit, Berry, and Nut Crops

   (a) Plant five fruit or nut trees, grapevines, or berry plants that are suited to your area. Take full care of fruit or nut trees, grapevines, or berry plants through one season.

   (b) Prune a tree, vine, or shrub properly. Explain why pruning is necessary.

   (c) Demonstrate one type of graft and tell why this method is useful.

   (d) Describe how one fruit, nut, or berry crop is processed for use.

3) Woody Ornamentals

   (a) Plant five or more trees or shrubs in a landscape setting. Take full care of the trees or shrubs you have planted for one growing season.

   (b) Prune a tree or shrub properly. Explain why pruning is necessary.

   (c) List 10 trees (in addition to those listed in general requirement 5 above) and tell your counselor how each is used in the landscape. Give the common and scientific names.

(d) Describe the size, texture, color, flowers, leaves, fruit, hardiness, cultural requirements, and any special characteristics that make each type of tree or shrub attractive or interesting.

(e) Tell five ways trees help improve the quality of our environment.

4) Home Gardening

(a) Design and plant a garden or landscape that is at least 10 by 10 feet.

(b) Plant 10 or more different types of plants in your garden. Tell why you selected particular varieties of vegetables and flowers. Take care of the plants in your garden for one season.

(c) Demonstrate soil preparation, staking, watering, weeding, mulching, composting, fertilizing, pest management, and pruning. Tell why each technique is used.

(d) Tell four types of things you could provide to make your home landscape or park a better place for birds and wildlife. List the common and scientific names of 10 kinds of native plants that are beneficial to birds and wildlife in your area.

Field Botany Option

A. Visit a park, forest, or other natural area near your home. While you are there:

1) Determine which species of plants are the largest and which are the most abundant. Note whether they cast shade on other plants.

2) Record environmental factors that may influence the presence of plants on your site, including latitude, climate, air and soil temperature, soil type and pH, geology, hydrology, and topography.

3) Record any differences in the types of plants you see at the edge of a forest, near water, in burned areas, or near a road or railroad.

B. Select a study site that is at least 100 by 100 feet. Make a list of the plants in the study site by groups of plants: canopy trees, small trees, shrubs, herbaceous wildflowers and grasses, vines, ferns, mosses, algae, fungi, lichens. Find out which of these are native plants and which are exotic (or nonnative).

C. Tell how an identification key works and use a simple key to identify 10 kinds of plants (in addition to those in general requirement 5 above). Tell the difference between common and scientific names and tell why scientific names are important.

D. After gaining permission, collect, identify, press, mount, and label 10 different plants that are common in your area. Tell why voucher specimens are important for documentation of a field botanist's discoveries.

E. Obtain a list of rare plants of your state. Tell what is being done to protect rare plants and natural areas in your state. Write a paragraph about one of the rare plants in your state.

F. Choose ONE of the following alternatives and complete EACH of its requirements:

1) Tree Inventory

(a) Identify the trees of your neighborhood or a park or section of your town.

(b) Collect, press, and label leaves, flowers, or fruits to document your inventory.

(c) List the types of trees by scientific name and give common names. Note the number and size (diameter at 4 feet above ground) of trees observed and determine the largest of each species in your study area.

(d) Lead a walk to teach others about trees and their value, OR write and distribute materials that will help others learn about trees.

2) Transect Study

   (a) Visit two sites, at least one of which is different from the one you visited for Field Botany requirement 1.

   (b) Use the transect method to study the two different kinds of plant communities. The transects should be at least 500 feet long.

   (c) At each site, record observations about the soil and other influencing factors AND do the following. Then make a graph or chart to show the results of your studies.

   (1) Identify each tree within 10 feet of the transect line.

   (2) Measure the diameter of each tree at 4 feet above the ground, and map and list each tree.

3) Nested Plot

   (a) Visit two sites, at least one of which is different from the one you visited for Field Botany requirement 1.

   (b) Mark off nested plots and inventory two different kinds of plant communities.

   (c) At each site, record observations about the soil and other influencing factors AND do the following. Then make a graph or chart to show the results of your studies.

   (1) Identify, measure, and map each tree in a 100-by-100-foot plot. (Measure the diameter of each tree at 4 feet above the ground.)

   (2) Identify and map all trees and shrubs in a 10-by-10-foot plot within each of the larger areas.

   (3) Identify and map all plants (wildflowers, ferns, grasses, mosses, etc.) of a 4-by-4-foot plot within the 10-by-10-foot plot.

4) Herbarium Visit

 (a) Write ahead and arrange to visit an herbarium at a university, park, or botanical garden; OR, visit an herbarium website (with your parent's permission).

 (b) Tell how the specimens are arranged and how they are used by researchers. If possible, observe voucher specimens of a plant that is rare in your state.

 (c) Tell how a voucher specimen is mounted and prepared for permanent storage. Tell how specimens should be handled so that they will not be damaged.

 (d) Tell about the tools and references used by botanists in an herbarium.

5) Plant Conservation Organization Visit

 (a) Write ahead and arrange to visit a private conservation organization or government agency that is concerned with protecting rare plants and natural areas.

 (b) Tell about the activities of the organization in studying and protecting rare plants and natural areas.

 (c) If possible, visit a nature preserve managed by the organization. Tell about land management activities such as controlled burning, or measures to eradicate invasive (nonnative) plants or other threats to the plants that are native to the area.

Contents

What Is Plant Science? 13

The World of Plants 15

Agronomy. 33

Horticulture. 55

Field Botany 79

Careers in Plant Science. 91

Plant Science Resources. 94

What Is Plant Science?

Have you ever wondered why the leaves on a tree change from green to yellow or red in the autumn, or why only certain types of plants grow in valleys, while other types of plants grow on mountains? If you have ever asked questions like these, then you are on your way to becoming a plant scientist.

All scientists ask questions about things they observe, then try to find answers. Plant scientists use their curiosity and knowledge to develop questions about the world of plants. Then they try to answer those questions with further observations and experiments in the laboratory and in the field. As you earn the Plant Science merit badge, you will develop a number of the skills plant scientists use.

Using This Pamphlet

Botany is the scientific study of plants. The field of botany encompasses more than a dozen specialties, including plant pathology, agronomy, plant taxonomy, horticulture, floriculture, paleobotany, forestry, and plant ecology. In this merit badge pamphlet, you will explore three of the most important plant science specialties—agronomy, horticulture, and field botany. You will work on activities and projects in each of these three areas of plant science and gain an appreciation for the important work that plant scientists do.

> **Farmers are plant scientists.** They observe how plants respond during the growing season, ask questions about why plants grow in certain ways, and adjust their farming methods to test their ideas for growing better crops.

The World of Plants

The world contains between 250,000 and 500,000 known species of plants and probably thousands more that have yet to be discovered and classified. You can find plant life almost everywhere in the world. Deserts, prairies, shorelines, and urban parks abound with a stunning variety of vegetation. Plant communities thrive in the mountains, too, and bring richness and variety to wetlands, woodlands, tundra, and forests.

Plant Divisions

Botanists have classified all plants as members of one of five large divisions—*mosses, club mosses, horsetails, ferns* and their allies, and *seed plants*. The following is a brief description of each of these plant divisions.

Mosses (Bryophytes)

Mosses are small plants, usually less than an inch tall, that grow in rock crevices, on forest floors and tree trunks, and along stream banks. They may have a small spore capsule at the end of a stalk that rises above a leafy base. Haircap moss, apple moss, and the closely related liverworts and hornworts are all mosses. Most of the mosses and their close relatives live on land.

Moss

Club Mosses (Lycopsids)

Club mosses differ from true mosses because they are *vascular*—that is, they have veins. In prehistoric times, they were far more prevalent than they are today. Present-day club mosses are small plants with needlelike leaves that often grow on the forest floor in tropical to temperate regions.

Club moss

THE WORLD OF PLANTS

Photosynthesis

All plants and animals need energy to keep them alive. Most plants absorb energy from sunlight, which they use to convert carbon dioxide, water, and soil nutrients into plant food. *Chlorophyll,* a chemical compound that makes most plants appear green to the human eye, uses the sun's energy to convert water and carbon dioxide into simple sugars called *carbohydrates.* This chemical process, called *photosynthesis,* also returns oxygen to the atmosphere.

Photosynthesis

carbon dioxide + water + sunlight ⟶ glucose (sugar) + oxygen + water

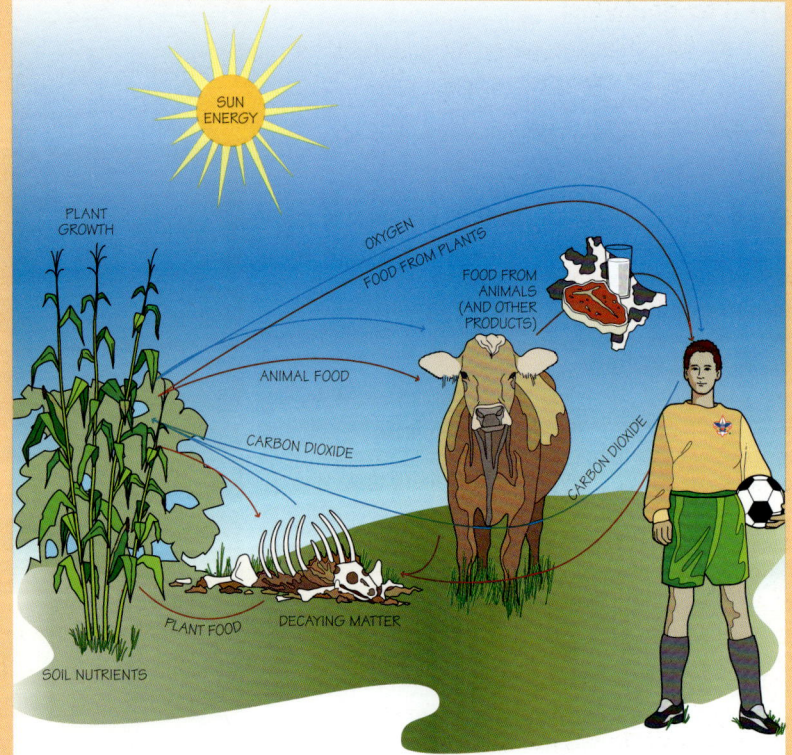

Green plants produce the oxygen that supports all of Earth's animal life, including human life.

Horsetails (Equisetophytes)

Horsetails are an ancient group of plants. They have hollow, jointed, and usually grooved stems. Cone-shaped structures atop the horsetail stems produce spores from which horsetails reproduce.

> During a single growing season, one mature broad-leaved tree (such as an oak or a cottonwood) can produce enough oxygen to keep 10 people alive for an entire year.

Horsetail

Ferns (Pteridophytes)

Ferns often have lacy leaves called *fronds*. Uncurling in the spring, the fronds of some ferns resemble the decorative ends of violins and thus are called *fiddleheads*. Ferns are most abundant in the shade of moist forests.

Seed Plants (Spermatophytes)

Seed plants make up the great majority of Earth's plants. Among them are the most ancient living organisms on the planet, the 4,000-year-old bristlecone pines, and some of the largest living organisms, the giant sequoias, which can weigh more than 6,000 tons. Seed plants are divided into two groups: nonflowering plants (gymnosperms) such as conifers, ginkgos, and ephedras, and flowering plants (angiosperms) such as wildflowers, grasses, and flowering trees and shrubs.

Fern, showing a fiddlehead

> **Extremely hungry:** More than 600 plant species are carnivorous, which means that they capture and digest insects and other small animals. The Venus flytrap snaps its leaves shut around insects that touch trigger hairs on the leaves. The insects are eventually digested by enzymes, providing nutrients for the plant.

Flowering plants

The World of Plants

Flowering Plants

All flowering plants share similar reproductive structures in their flowers. The following cross section shows the major parts of a typical flower.

ANTHER
The structure at the end of the filament that contains pollen grains.

POLLEN
The dustlike particles that pollinate the flower. Pollen is often carried by wind or insects to the pistil.

PETAL
The large, often brightly colored and fragrant flower petals occurring just above the sepals.

FILAMENT
The thin stalk that supports the anther.

STIGMA
The top surface of the pistil that receives the pollen.

STYLE
The tubelike structure that connects the stigma to the ovary.

STAMEN
The male part of the flower, consisting of the filament, anther, and pollen.

SEPAL
The layer of small leaves at the base of the flower, just beneath the whorl of petals.

PISTIL
The female part of the flower, consisting of the stigma, style, and ovary.

OVULES
The area surrounded by the ovary that develops into seeds.

OVARY
The bottom of the pistil, beneath the style, that surrounds the ovule. The ovary develops into the fruit of the plant.

Parts of the flowering plant

THE WORLD OF PLANTS

The Buzz About Bees

Did you realize that much of our existence depends on honeybees? We rely on them not only for honey, but more importantly, for their ability to pollinate many of the crops we eat and the feed farmers give their livestock. Without honeybees, our food sources would be significantly reduced. They contribute significantly in three ways:

- Honeybees are nature's most efficient pollinators. They visit only one kind of flower on each foraging trip, so they transfer only pollen that flower can use.

- A colony produces thousands of pollinators each season, creating a workforce unrivaled by other pollinating species.

- Honeybees can be raised in hives made by humans, and those hives can be transported to areas where their pollination skills are needed.

Pollination by honeybees is vital to humankind. Although birds, bats, bumblebees, butterflies, and many other creatures help transfer pollen as they flit from flower to flower or feed on the nectar of several flowers, the honeybee pollinates with a purpose. Our world and eating habits would be very different without the honeybee to pollinate our plants.

Many of the fresh fruits and vegetables we enjoy today would not survive or exist without the help of the honeybee. Farmers would worry about the availability of many of the feeds for their animals. Cows, horses, chickens, and pigs all eat feeds pollinated by the honeybee. So, next time you see a honeybee in action, busy pollinating, leave it alone and let it do its thing.

PLANT SCIENCE

Why Plants Are Important

Plants and plant communities are essential to human life. Here are a few of the many ways that plants are important to humans.

- **Plants let us breathe.** Plants produce oxygen as a by-product of photosynthesis. Without plants, animals—including humans—could not exist on Earth.
- **Plants keep us healthy.** Almost half of the medicines we use were developed from wild plants. The chemicals in many species of plants have been extracted and analyzed by plant scientists. These chemicals are the raw materials of the medicines you get from your doctor or pharmacist to help prevent or treat illness.
- **Plants feed us.** Green plants convert the energy of the sun into food, which is stored in plant leaves, stems, seeds, fruits, and roots. About a dozen plant species, including rice, wheat, corn, and potatoes, account for almost all of the food that humans consume. Because animals eat plants, plants are indirectly responsible for many other foods people eat, such as meat, fish, milk, and eggs.
- **Plants protect the soil and water.** The deep roots of shrubs, grasses, trees, and wildflowers hold soil in place during rainstorms. Without plant cover, soil can quickly erode and may wash into streams and lakes, causing pollution.
- **Plants keep us cool.** The world's plants absorb sunlight and provide shade. Plants also absorb carbon dioxide, a gas that may cause Earth's temperature to increase. The plants in the Amazon rain forest in South America absorb a tremendous amount of the world's carbon dioxide gas. Many scientists believe that global warming will increase if the plants in the world's forests are not preserved.
- **Plants give us wild places.** The meadows, forests, and deserts are filled with plants that provide habitat for wild animals. They also provide us with opportunities for hiking, camping, and wildlife and flower photography.
- **Plants give us shelter.** Most people in the world use plant materials to build their houses. Wood from trees is the most common building material in much of the world. To help protect our dwindling supply of trees, other plant materials are now being used inside homes, including the stems of the bamboo plant and pressed wheat stems.

Plant-Naming Systems

Plants are often identified by their common names, but common names can vary from region to region. For example, the wildflower jack-in-the-pulpit is also known as the Indian turnip. To avoid confusion, scientists follow a universal naming system that uses Latin terms to describe each plant species. For example, botanists would refer to jack-in-the-pulpit by its scientific name, *Arisaema triphyllum*. The first part of the name identifies the *genus* (a general group of closely related species) and the second part of the name identifies the *species* (a specific kind of plant with similar characteristics). Without this system, it would be impossible for scientists to be certain that they were discussing the same plant.

The Nature and Function of Soil

Soil is so familiar to us that we seldom give it a second thought, but it is more complex than you may think. It consists of mineral matter (a mix of silt, sand, and clay), water, air, and dead and living organic material (plant roots, bacteria, fungi, nematodes, protozoa, arthropods, and earthworms).

Soil Composition

Most soils begin their development from various kinds of rock. Over thousands of years, sun, wind, rain, and other natural forces break down rock into smaller and smaller pieces, eventually grinding them into tiny particles. But these small rock particles do not become soil until they combine with once-living plants and animals—organic matter. Soil owes its structure to organic matter, which creates spaces in the soil for moisture and air.

Soil scientists have identified more than 70,000 kinds of soil in the United States. Climate, the rock from which the soil formed, plant and animal life, topography, and time all affect the development of soils and cause soils to be different. Particularly important is the climate, especially temperature and precipitation. Climate determines how fast and in what way rocks break down and what kinds of plants grow in a particular place. In turn, the kinds of plants that grow (and how fast they decay) and the activity of soil organisms determine the kind of soil that develops.

Soil Texture

When soil experts refer to soil texture, they are talking about the proportion and size of the three different types of solid mineral particles it contains: sand, silt, and clay. To determine soil texture, rub some soil between your fingers. If the soil feels coarse and gritty and you can just barely see individual particles, it must contain a large proportion of sand—particles that range from 0.05 millimeters to 2.0 millimeters in diameter.

Silty soil feels smooth, like flour. Moisten some soil and work it into a thin ribbon between your thumb and forefinger. If the ribbon breaks off near your fingers when you try to lengthen it, chances are the soil is largely silt. Particles in a silty soil typically range from 0.002 to 0.05 millimeters in diameter. You cannot see the individual soil particles in a silty soil without using a strong magnifying glass.

THE WORLD OF PLANTS

Nature's forces slowly crumble rocks into mineral particles of clay, sand, and silt.

A clay soil will feel like fine powder when dry. After you moisten it, you will be able to make at least an inchlong ribbon when you rub it between your fingers. Clay soil contains soil particles smaller than silt and less than 0.002 millimeters in diameter.

When a soil is identified as a *loam* (this term refers only to the size of particles the soil contains), it means that the soil contains a relatively even mixture of sand and silt and a somewhat smaller proportion of clay. Plants grow very well in loamy soil.

Soil Structure

Soil particles tend to cling together to form larger clumps of soil. These clusters are called *peds* or *aggregates,* and the way they group together is the soil structure. Organic matter—bacteria, plant roots, fungi, and earthworm slime—is what helps soil

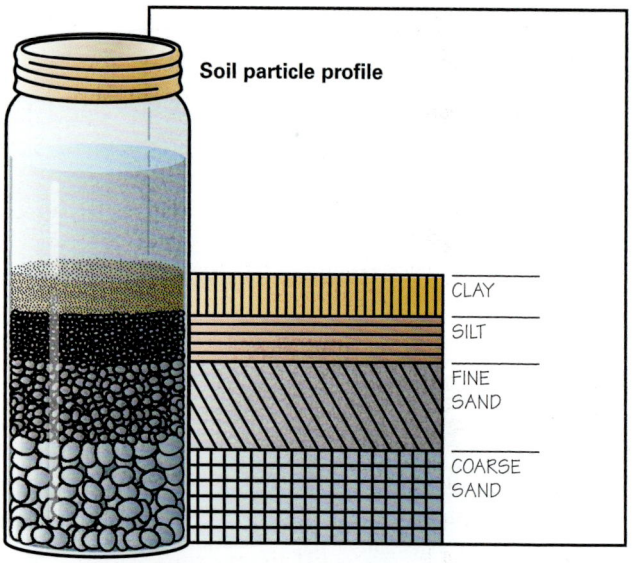

Soil particle profile

Try this experiment. Fill a jar two-thirds full of water and pour in a cup of soil. Shake it vigorously and then let it stand for several hours. Hold a piece of paper against the side of the jar and draw a diagram of the layers to make your own soil chart. Do the layers look like these? Explain why the largest particles settle on the bottom.

Major Types of Soil Structures

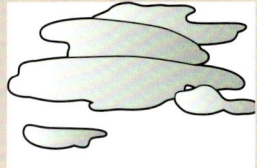

PLATY

Flat, thin, flaky layers in soil. Slow rate of water infiltration.

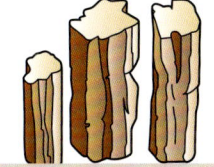

PRISMATIC

Vertical columns in soil that may be several inches long and $1/2$ to 2 inches in diameter. Moderate rate of infiltration.

BLOCKY

Angular blocks $1/2$ to 2 inches in diameter. Moderate rate of infiltration.

GRANULAR OR CRUMB

Like a crumbly cake. The crumbs or grains are usually less than $1/4$ inch in diameter. Rapid rate of infiltration. This soil structure is usually best for growing plants because it has many pores for water and air.

GRAVEL OR SAND

Loose, rounded particles that do not stick together. Rapid rate of infiltration.

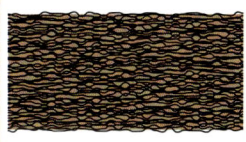

HEAVY OR MASSIVE

Large clods of clumping soil. No visible structure. The clods are difficult to break apart. Slow rate of infiltration.

A soil's structure may change over the years. For example, a fertile crumb soil may deteriorate into a heavy or massive soil if it is continuously tilled or if livestock constantly trample it.

clump together. Some very loose soils, such as beach sand, do not clump at all, but rather consist of single grains instead of structured soil.

A soil's structure is important because it determines how well that soil allows plants to access water, nutrients, and air. The best soils for most plants are those that let water infiltrate, or soak in, at a moderate rate.

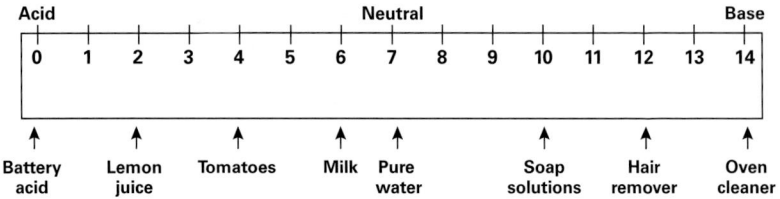

The pH of some common substances is shown on this pH scale.

Soil pH

A scientific measurement called the *pH scale* is used to measure the acidity and alkalinity of a soil. On the pH scale, a value of zero indicates extremely strong acidity, while a value of 14.0 indicates extreme alkalinity. A soil with a pH of 7.0, midway between zero and 14.0, represents a neutral soil. Certain plants, such as blueberries, grow best in somewhat acidic soils with a pH of 4.5; roses, as well as most annual flowers and vegetables, grow best in a neutral to slightly acidic soil; farm crops thrive best in soils ranging from pH 6.0 to 8.0. Very few plants will grow in soils with a pH higher than 10.0 or lower than 3.5.

Plant Nutrients and Soil Fertility

Plants need three major chemical elements to thrive—nitrogen, phosphorus, and potassium. In addition, plants also need very small amounts of sulfur, calcium, iron, manganese, magnesium, molybdenum, boron, copper, zinc, and a few other trace elements. Even though most plants need only a small amount of these elements, their presence is essential. Most plant nutrients are located in the top layer of soil. If some of these elements are lacking in the soil, they can be added through the use of natural or chemical fertilizers.

One way to maintain soil fertility is by rotating crops (planting different crops on a piece of land in a planned sequence from year to year), adding lime to soils to reduce acidity, adding manure, and growing cover crops (such as alfalfa and clover). Another way to increase fertility is to add *compost* to the soil. Compost is a rich soil conditioner consisting of rotted organic matter such as leaves, grass clippings, dead garden plants, vegetable scraps, and other plant material. When this organic matter decomposes over a period of about six months, it breaks down into phosphorus, nitrogen, sulfur, and other compounds that vegetation needs to thrive.

An added benefit of composting is that waste is recycled instead of being dumped in a landfill.

26 **PLANT SCIENCE**

= THE WORLD OF PLANTS

> **Extremely heavy:** A single giant sequoia tree in California weighs more than 8 million pounds. It would take the combined weight of 30 blue whales— the heaviest animal on Earth—to equal the weight of one giant sequoia tree.

Plant Propagation

Propagation means reproduction. Although most propagation of plants is by seed, plants also can reproduce in other ways. In addition to seed propagation, plants can reproduce from roots, tubers, cuttings, and grafts.

Propagation by Seed

Seed propagation is a form of sexual reproduction. Both the male and the female elements of a plant's flower must join together to create a new seed. Many of the seeds used today in crop production were developed by plant scientists through cross-fertilization. Plant scientists discovered that taking the pollen from one variety of a plant and using that pollen to fertilize the stigma of another variety of the same plant could produce a different plant variety that would have the best qualities of both parent plants.

Propagation by Roots

Certain plants can be reproduced by simply planting portions of the plant roots in moist soil or in a jar of water. You can demonstrate root propagation with a sweet potato, which is really the root of the plant.

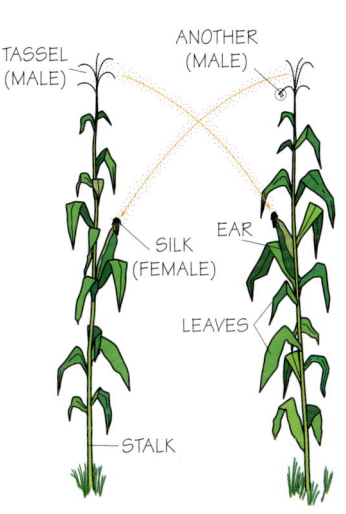

In simplified form, the cross-fertilization of corn plants

PLANT SCIENCE 27

PROPAGATING A SWEET POTATO

Put a fresh sweet potato in a glass jar filled with water. Leave about a third of the sweet potato exposed. Stick toothpicks in the side of the sweet potato, with the ends of the toothpicks extending over the jar rim to balance the potato, so it is partially submerged in water. Set the jar in a warm, sunny spot such as a window ledge. Replace the water in the jar once a week, making sure the water level doesn't drop below the bottom of the potato. In two to three weeks, roots will appear on the submerged portion of the sweet potato, and leaves will sprout above the water line. If you keep filling the jar with water, these leaves will develop into vines that can grow up to several feet long over four to six months.

Propagation by Tubers

A sweet potato is the root of the plant, but a white potato is an example of a tuber, the enlarged, fleshy growth of an underground stem. White potatoes can be grown from seeds, but many gardeners and commercial growers instead plant cut-up pieces of potatoes, with each piece containing the eyes, or buds, of the potato. These potato pieces are called *seed potatoes*. You can propagate your own potato tubers by cutting up chunks of a large potato, ensuring that each piece has two or more eyes. Plant the potato chunks at least 2 inches deep in gardening pots filled with potting soil. Keep the soil moist and warm. After a few weeks, you should see a new potato plant emerging from the soil.

Extremely big: The giant "double coconut" seeds of the coco-de-mer palm are found on the Seychelles, a thousand miles off the coast of Africa. The monster seed can grow more than a foot long and weigh 40 pounds.

THE WORLD OF PLANTS

Propagation Using Cuttings

Many gardeners propagate plants by cutting stems or leaves and planting them directly in a soil mix. The new plants are genetically identical to the source plant, and they grow to maturity faster than those started from seeds. The following diagram shows how to plant cuttings of stems and leaves of such plants as juniper, strawberry, rose, ivy, azalea, carnation, and geranium.

Steps for Propagating Using Plant Cuttings

Step 1—Cut off a leafy stem about 6 inches long from the donor plant.

Step 2—Strip off all but a few leaves at the tip of the stem.

Step 3—Plant the cutting in a container filled with a layer of gravel on the bottom followed by a good rooting soil mixture, leaving about one-third of the height of the stem above the soil.

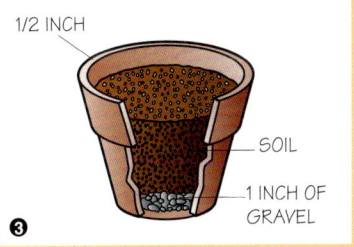

Step 4—Cover the soil container with a plastic bag and put it in a light, warm place—but not in direct sunlight. Keep the soil moist.

In two to four weeks, most plant cuttings will have sent down roots, and the newly rooted cuttings will be ready for transplanting.

You also can start new plants from leaf cuttings. Some leaf cuttings will start in water; others are started in a bed of moist sand. When the roots sent down from the leaf are about 1 inch long, the young plant can be planted in moist soil.

The World of Plants

Propagation by Grafting

Grafting is a form of propagation in which parts of two different plants are joined together to make a new plant. Grafting is discussed in the horticulture section of this merit badge pamphlet.

Native Plants, Exotics, and Weeds

Native plants are the natural inhabitants of an area. An *exotic*, or nonnative, plant is one that has been introduced to an area. Some nonnative plants spread aggressively, invading crops and pushing out native species important to wildlife. Such invasive plants are often designated as weeds. A *noxious* plant is a weed designated by law as undesirable and requiring control. Noxious plants are usually nonnative and are highly invasive.

Many native plants have fibrous root systems that provide soil cover, stability, and water infiltration, while many weeds have narrow taproots that leave bare soil exposed to erosion. Other weeds have roots that penetrate deeper than those of native plants, allowing them to tap more water and thus crowd out native vegetation.

Weed seeds can be spread by wind, water, livestock, wildlife, vehicles, and people. People traveling with horses, mules, or other livestock in the backcountry often carry hay that is specially treated to prevent weed seeds from taking root.

Noxious plants in the United States include purple loosestrife *(left),* Scotch broom, and spotted knapweed.

Controlling Invasive Weeds

Among the most labor-intensive challenges facing landowners is the spread of weeds. Consider using this four-part plan to control weed outbreaks.

- **Prevention**—Educate yourself on ways to avoid transporting weed seeds from one area to another.

- **Removal**—Remove weeds from an area, using natural control methods whenever possible.

- **Restoration**—Help native vegetation reestablish itself.

- **Monitoring**—Seek out and eliminate new weed growth.

Here are some guidelines to follow if you decide to remove invasive weeds.

- Properly identify the plant you think is a weed. If you are not sure, do not remove it until it has been identified.

- Pull weeds at the right time of the year—ideally before they produce seed.

- Wear long-sleeved shirts, long pants, and gloves when working with weeds that have thorns or sap that can irritate the skin.

- Pull small infestations of weeds by hand, especially when a noxious plant has first been detected in an area. Hand-pulling also is a good alternative in sites where *herbicides* (chemical weed killers) and mechanical removal methods cannot be used.

- If weeds have deep root systems and cannot be pulled out by hand, try cutting them flush with the ground or using shovels or other tools to dig them out of the ground.

- Properly dispose of the weeds that you remove. Some plant parts and weed seeds can spread and reestablish the weed if left on the ground.

Agronomy

Plant scientists who study how to produce field crops for food, fiber, or forage are called *agronomists*. Agronomists include farmers who raise crops as well as crop scientists who conduct field studies and laboratory experiments. The goal of the agronomist is to produce higher-quality crops more efficiently and to develop methods to control crop pests. The work of agronomists is essential for humans as well as for Earth's environmental health. Three grain crops—wheat, rice, and corn—make up the majority of the food we eat, either through direct consumption or as feed for cattle, hogs, or other animals we eat as meat. Agronomists study how to produce these important crops with fewer chemicals, higher yields, and more nutritional value. Agronomists also work to find new plant species that can be adapted for food production.

Chief Growing Regions for Major Crops

Corn. More than 10 billion bushels of corn are produced every year in the United States—more than twice as much as any other crop. Corn grows best in climates with warm, sunny days and lots of moisture. Most corn production is centered in Iowa, Illinois, Minnesota, Indiana, and Nebraska. The majority of corn produced in the nation is used for feeding livestock such as cattle and hogs. Other uses of corn include the production of high-fructose corn syrup, which is used to sweeten food, and ethanol, which often is added to gasoline.

Agronomy

Soybeans. More than 2 billion bushels of soybeans are produced yearly in the United States—more than 40 percent of the world's soybean crop. Like corn, soybeans are produced primarily in the Midwest, with Iowa, Illinois, Indiana, Ohio, and Minnesota leading production. Soybeans grow best in warm, sunny weather, with daytime temperatures between 80 and 90 degrees. While the United States is the world's largest producer of soybeans, Brazil has been rapidly increasing its soybean production and is now a close second.

The trend in soybean production is toward planting in narrow rows. The leaves form a canopy and shade the soil between the rows, limiting the growth of weeds. Another advantage is that the pods form higher on plants that are densely populated because the sunlight doesn't reach the lower parts of the plant. That reduces crop losses that result when the harvesting machines miss the low-growing bean pods.

Soybeans are a great source of low-fat protein. More than 90 percent of the U.S. soybean crop is used to feed livestock, but soybeans are an increasingly popular food for humans. Some of the more common foods produced from soybeans include soybean milk, tofu, soy flour, and soybean oil.

AGRONOMY

Cotton. The United States grows about one-fifth of the world's cotton. Leading the nation in cotton production are the states of Texas, California, Arkansas, Georgia, Mississippi, Arizona, Louisiana, and North Carolina. Cotton is grown in a variety of climates, including the humid Mississippi Delta, the West Texas High Plains, and the deserts of the Southwest. Cotton needs long, hot days and a good water supply, which is often provided through irrigation.

In the United States, all commercial cotton is harvested by machine. A one-row cotton stripper can harvest 500 pounds of cotton in an hour; a person can pick only 15 pounds in the same time. The cotton stripper slices the bolls and some of the leaves from the stalk. Growers try to keep trash (leaves, stems, boll husks) out of the harvest because they earn more money for clean, top-graded cotton. Another machine, the cotton picker, pulls the cotton from the bolls. The cotton ginning machines separate cottonseeds from the fiber. They also dry, clean, and package the cotton into bales before it is delivered to textile mills.

Cotton fiber is used in many items of clothing, including blue jeans and T-shirts. Cottonseeds also are a valuable product of the cotton harvest. Cottonseeds are pressed to make cottonseed oil, which is used in cooking and soap-making.

A single 500-pound bale of cotton contains enough cotton fiber to make more than 200 pairs of jeans.

PLANT SCIENCE

A legume converts nitrogen found in the atmosphere into more complex nitrogen compounds such as ammonia and nitrates. These complex nitrogen compounds are natural fertilizers and help enrich the soil to promote better plant growth.

Forage crops. Forage crops are plants other than grain that are raised specifically for feeding to grazing or browsing livestock, such as cattle, sheep, and horses. Forage crops include many perennial grasses, such as timothy, fescue, and bromegrass, and cover crops like alfalfa and clover.

Alfalfa and clover are legumes that are often planted to help increase the fertility of soil. Although legumes enrich soil, they also can deplete the soil's productivity after a few years of continuous planting. This depletion occurs because legumes need phosphorus for their own growth. Legumes eventually may reduce the phosphorus available in the soil. Legumes also need lots of water to grow and can deplete water supplies in soil over time. Farmers often alternate plant species from year to year to restore the soil's nutrients that have been depleted by previous plantings.

Alfalfa is grown in every state. It is the third most valuable crop in the United States, exceeded only by corn and soybeans in total crop value. The yearly value of the nation's alfalfa crop exceeds $8 billion.

Forage Crops as Feed

Farmers make hay, meal, and silage from forage crops.

Hay. Grass, alfalfa, or clover cut and dried as a bulky feed given to livestock for roughage.

Meal. Coarsely ground unsifted edible seeds produced by legume crops.

Silage. Succulent feed produced by storing a forage crop in an airtight silo and allowing it to ferment. Silage is easier to digest and is fed to dairy cows.

AGRONOMY

Small grains. Small grains (often called cereal grains) include wheat, rice, oats, barley, and rye. Wheat and rice are the two most important small grain crops in the United States.

Wheat. Two main types of wheat are planted in the United States—spring wheat and winter wheat. Spring wheat, planted in April and May, is harvested in August and September. Spring wheat does best in climates where the summers are fairly mild. Most of the nation's spring wheat crop is grown in the far northern states of North Dakota, South Dakota, Minnesota, and Montana. Winter wheat, which grows best in states with a mild winter, is planted in the fall. The winter wheat seeds sprout before the winter cold sets in. The sprouted wheat then spends the winter months under a blanket of snow, which provides insulation from cold temperatures that could harm or kill the tender plants. As the spring sun warms the soil, winter wheat quickly reemerges. It is harvested in early summer. Most of the nation's winter wheat crop is grown in Kansas, Oklahoma, and Washington.

Rice. More than 2 billion people in the world, especially those in Asia and India, get the majority of their daily calories from eating rice. The major rice-producing countries are China, India, Indonesia, and Bangladesh. These four countries produce nearly 70 percent of the world's rice supply. In the United States, rice is grown in the southern states. Arkansas alone accounts for close to half of the nation's rice crop. California, Texas, Louisiana, and Mississippi are also important rice-producing states. Rice is a semiaquatic plant, and rice fields are kept flooded with 6 to 8 inches of water until just before harvest.

PLANT SCIENCE

AGRONOMY

How to Find Crop Production Statistics

The United States Department of Agriculture (USDA) maintains the National Agricultural Statistics Service Reports website, http://www.nass.usda.gov, which features yearly production figures for more than a dozen crops, including wheat, barley, corn, alfalfa, rice, soybeans, fruits, and nuts. You can also check the *U.S. Statistical Report* or *Agricultural Statistics Handbook,* both of which may be available at your public library. If you need help, ask your merit badge counselor or county extension agent to access these statistics for you.

Small Grain Production and Harvests

To improve production, farmers try to select the best small grain varieties. High-quality seeds produce a greater yield. Growers are concerned about disease resistance, grain quality, straw strength, and plant height. If crops are tall and weak, they may become *lodged,* or flattened down, by storms or cultivation.

Closely grown small grain crops quickly develop a vegetative cover that protects the soil from wind and water erosion. Fall-planted crops, such as winter wheat and rye, prevent many spring weeds species from germinating. When small grain crops are rotated with row crops like corn, cotton, and soybeans, the overall erosion rate for the rotation decreases. Farmers may limit how much they disturb the soil by reducing the number of tillage trips across the field. Commercial equipment can plant seed well into the remaining crop stubble.

Another way to reduce harvest losses is to use artificial drying facilities to remove moisture from small grains. Good storage management will prevent spoilage caused by mold growth and insect activity.

Germination Testing

No crop can be better than its seed. In any bag of seeds, some will not be *viable;* that is, they will not grow. Before farmers plant a field crop, they need to determine how many of the purchased seeds will *germinate,* or sprout. Calculating the germination rate of seeds helps a farmer know how many seeds need to be planted to ensure a successful harvest.

Conduct Your Own Seed-Germination Test

Step 1—Thoroughly moisten one paper towel and lay it flat on a table.

Step 2—Place 50 seeds of one plant species on a wet paper towel in 10 rows, with five seeds per row. Make sure that the seeds are not touching each other. (Ungerminated seeds can get moldy and cause normal seeds to lose their sprouting ability.)

Step 3—Moisten a second paper towel and place it on top of the rows of seeds. Press down gently on the top paper towel to make sure it is touching all the seeds.

Step 4—Gently roll the paper towel and seeds into the shape of a tube.

Step 5—Place the rolled-up tube in a plastic bag, and seal the bag. Place the sealed bag in a warm area (on top of your refrigerator or on your kitchen table).

Step 6—After a couple of days, open the bag and make sure that the paper towels are still moist. If they are starting to dry out, sprinkle some more water on the paper towels, and then reseal the bag.

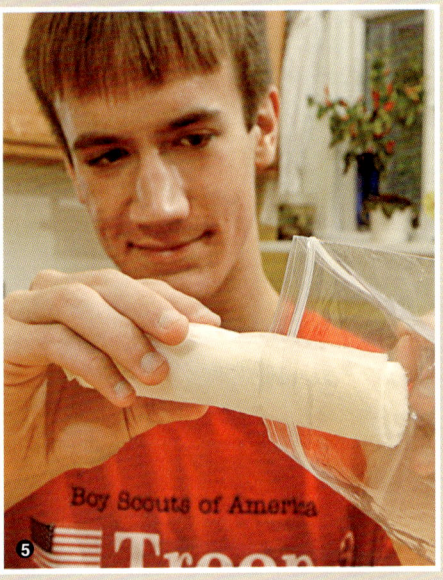

Step 7—Check the bag once a week to see if the germination is completed. Most plant seeds will germinate within one to three weeks.

Step 8—When you are certain that the germination is finished, count all the seeds that have germinated, and then divide this number by the total number of seeds you tested to determine the germination rate. For instance, if 40 seeds sprout in a test of 50 seeds, then the germination rate is 40 divided by 50, which equals an 80 percent germination rate. An acceptable germination rate for certified corn or soybean seeds is typically above 90 percent.

Step 9—Repeat this germination test for three other plant species, using fresh paper towels.

Raising Your Own Plot of Field Crops

To successfully raise a plot of field crops, you will need to plan the size and location of your plot, prepare the seedbed, plant and water your crop, deal with insect pests and weeds, and harvest the mature crop. Farmers spend the winter months planning their spring planting. The winter months are also the best time for you to do your planning for raising your own plot of field crops.

One of the first things you should do in your planning is contact your merit badge counselor or county extension agent. You also might contact local farmers, vocational agriculture teachers from high schools or community colleges, or a chapter of the Future Farmers of America (FFA). These experts can provide you with specific information on growing field crops that are specifically adapted to your local climate.

Corn, soybeans, cotton, and other field crops all have different growing seasons, seedbed preparation requirements, and moisture requirements.

Your merit badge counselor, extension agent, or other advisor can give you advice on the size and location of your plot, seedbed preparation, and many other practical matters. Plan a meeting with your merit badge counselor or extension agent a month or two before the local growing season starts so you have time to get everything ready.

Your advisors also can help you with specific growing issues, such as the proper planting date for your crop. For example, soybeans are best planted in soil that is warmer than 50 degrees, temperatures that usually occur in May or June in the Midwest. Planting soybeans earlier than this runs the risk of the emergent soybeans encountering a killing frost. Cold temperatures (below 32 degrees) will freeze the water in plant cells and kill young soybeans. Farmers who plant too early sometimes have to replant an entire field if a late spring frost kills their young soybean plants.

> During the growing season, continue to seek advice from your expert advisors. The most successful farmers consult with agronomic experts and are constantly learning new farming techniques. Good farmers learn not only from their successes, but also from their failures. They try to apply what they learn from their harvests to produce a better crop the next growing season.

Controlling Weeds, Insects, and Poisonous Plants in Field Crops

The damage that insects and weeds cause to field crops and stored grain runs into the tens of billions of dollars each year in the United States. Wherever field crops are growing, you can be sure that insects and weeds either are in the field already or are trying to gain access to the crop. Poisonous plants that invade fields of forage crops are another problem for farmers, because livestock can become ill or even die after eating forage contaminated with poisonous plants. Agronomists spend much of their research time and dollars finding new ways to reduce the damage of insects, weeds, and poisonous plants on field crop production.

AGRONOMY

> Many insects and plants are actually beneficial to crops. Only a small percentage of insects and plants cause damage. Many insect species pollinate crops, while others prey on other pests that are harmful to crops. Weeds, too, sometimes have a useful function. Some weeds are left as a cover crop to help reduce soil erosion, to retain soil nutrients, and to provide forage for animals.

Each field crop and climate region attracts different species of poisonous plants, weeds, and insect pests. Your local county extension agent will have identification guides and control guidelines for the pest species that are most common in the field crops in your area. A few of the more common insect pests, poisonous plants, and weeds that infest field crops are described on the following pages.

Insects Harmful to Field Crops

European corn borer. The European corn borer is responsible for more than $1 billion in damage to corn crops each year, making it the most costly insect pest in the United States. The adult European corn borer is a small moth that lays eggs on the underside of the corn plant's leaves. When the eggs hatch, the *larvae* (caterpillars) burrow into and consume all parts of the corn plant, including the corn ears.

> **Extremely poisonous:** Ricin, an extract from the castor bean, is 12,000 times more poisonous than rattlesnake venom.

Grasshopper. All plants are food for some of the many species of grasshoppers. When conditions are just right, grasshopper populations can explode, and large clouds of grasshoppers (and locusts) can descend on a field crop, consuming entire crops of alfalfa, cotton, corn, and other grains. Major outbreaks of grasshoppers occurred in the United States in the late 1800s and the 1930s.

Grasshopper

Cotton boll weevil. The cotton boll weevil can do major damage to cotton crops. It is a gray or brown insect that is native to Mexico and Central America. Adult weevils are between $1/8$ inch and $1/2$ inch long. The adult female lays eggs in cotton buds or fruit, and when the eggs hatch, the larvae feed on the buds, destroying them. They mature into adults that also eat and destroy buds and bolls. Insect-control programs have eradicated the boll weevil from certain states where it was once a problem pest.

Cotton boll weevil

Army cutworm. Corn, alfalfa, wheat, soybeans, and many other crops provide food for army cutworms. These insects kill plants by eating the leaves and cutting off the stems at or just above the ground line. Most plant damage occurs when the army cutworm is in the larval stage. Look for small green or brown caterpillars on plant foliage. The adult insect is a moth. Army cutworms are found throughout the United States east of the Rocky Mountains and in California, New Mexico, and Arizona.

Army moth (top) and cutworm

Common Plant Diseases

Serious crop losses may occur if a crop becomes infected with a plant disease. Plant diseases may be caused by bacteria, fungi, or viruses. Diseases are controlled through the use of disease-resistant varieties of seeds and plants, crop rotation, or treatment with chemicals such as fungicides.

Bacterial diseases are caused by single-celled organisms that feed on plants. The host plant becomes diseased because the bacteria take nutrients from and cause damage to the host plant.

Fungal diseases are caused by multicelled, threadlike organisms called *fungi*. Fungi grow and produce spores that are carried by wind, insects, or water. Fungal infections damage the plant structure. Once weakened by fungal infection, a plant becomes vulnerable to other diseases. Plant scientists have bred varieties of many types of plants to be resistant to fungal diseases.

Viral diseases usually are spread by insects that carry the virus. When an insect feeds on plant leaves or stems, the virus enters the plant and begins to reproduce. Plants infected with viral diseases may grow deformed leaves, flowers, or fruit and may change color.

Common Plant Diseases in the United States

Wilt diseases. When plants wilt in large areas in a field during hot and dry periods, it is often caused by the weather. But when one plant turns yellow or wilts while the one next to it remains green and healthy, it may indicate a wilt disease. Wilt diseases may be caused by either fungi or bacteria. Corn wilt is a bacterial wilt, which is spread by flea beetles that have the bacteria in their bodies. When feeding on corn, the beetles transmit the bacteria to the corn.

Oak wilt

Fungal wilt is responsible for wilt diseases of many plant species. The fungi can live for many years in the soil and cause widespread destruction of cotton, tomato, strawberry, and many other crops. One way to control wilt diseases is to plant resistant varieties of the crops. Another method is crop rotation, in which different crop species that are not susceptible to the wilt disease are planted in the infected soil for several years.

AGRONOMY

Leaf spots

Leaf spots. These fungal diseases appear as black, brown, or gray spots on leaves, stems, and fruit. Various types of leaf spots affect wheat, barley, oats, corn, and cotton.

Smuts. These diseases, caused by fungi, produce swollen white to gray blisters or boils filled with black spores on leaves, stems, and seed of corn, wheat, oats, and grasses. When the blisters break open, the black spores are spread by wind.

Smuts

Rust. Many of the rust diseases are caused by unusual fungi that spend part of their lives on one host and part on another, producing orange or brown pustules on each host plant. The wheat rust fungus can alternate between the wheat and the barberry plant, costing millions of dollars in wheat crop losses. Rusts also affect barley, oats, and rye. Control of rust has been achieved through the introduction of rust-resistant grain strains.

Rust

PLANT SCIENCE

Agronomy

Sow thistle

Wild mustard

Quackgrass

Common Weeds Harmful to Crop Plants

Farmers spend billions every year to control the hundreds of weed species that compete with crop plants for nutrients and moisture. Here are a few of the most common weeds that infest field crops.

Sow thistle *(Sonchus arvensis).* There are several varieties of sow thistle, all of which have strong roots that spread rapidly. The sow thistle has a bright yellow flower similar to dandelions.

Wild mustard *(Sinapis arvensis).* Wild mustard, also known as charlock mustard, is easily recognized by its four petals that form a cross. The leaves of wild mustard are lobed, or notched, with small hairs on the underside of the leaves. Wild mustard is an invasive weed in a variety of field crops, alfalfa, and other forage crops. Besides being a weed, wild mustard can poison livestock if they eat a large quantity of the mustard seeds.

Quackgrass *(Elymus repens).* A widespread weed, quackgrass is difficult to control because it grows from underground roots that live for several years. These roots constantly send out new shoots, so the weed spreads rapidly. Quackgrass grows in a wide variety of habitats, including crop fields and pastures throughout the United States. Like many other weeds, quackgrass competes with cultivated crops for nutrients, sunlight, and water.

AGRONOMY

Canada thistle *(Cirsium arvense)*.
A serious invasive weed in many areas, this robust plant has deep, creeping roots. Canada thistle is a large plant, growing from 1 to 5 feet high. Its flowers are a deep purple. Large colonies of Canada thistle will spread from a single plant, crowding out native plants and field crops.

Redroot pigweed *(Amaranthus retroflexus)*. Redroot pigweed is common in all parts of the United States. Its roots are reddish or pinkish in color, with oval leaves that narrow at the tip. Pigweeds compete in soybean and cornfields for nutrients and water, which can reduce crop yields.

Spotted knapweed *(Centaurea biebersteinii)*. Spotted knapweed is an invasive plant that has ruined millions of acres of grazing land in the western United States. The purple or pink flowers occur on the end of narrow-branched stems with short, hairy leaves. The fast-growing plant crowds out native grasses and other forage plants. It is difficult to control, since it produces thousands of seeds and has a deep taproot that can regenerate even if the part of the plant above ground is removed.

PLANT SCIENCE

Livestock and Poisonous Plants

Cattle, sheep, and other livestock depend on farmers and ranchers to protect them from poisonous plants in their pastures and feedlots. Every year up to 5 percent of all horses, cattle, and sheep that graze pastures in the western United States become ill or die from eating poisonous plants. Ranchers and farmers need a thorough knowledge of poisonous plants so they can identify and eliminate them.

Common Poisonous Plants Dangerous to Livestock

Purple locoweed

Purple locoweed *(Oxytropis lambertii).* There are hundreds of species of locoweed, but only about two dozen are considered poisonous. The bright purple flowers of purple locoweed appear in 2- to 4-inch spikes close to the ground, surrounded by leaflets covered with silvery-white hairs. Purple locoweed contains chemical compounds that, if eaten, affect the nervous system of livestock, causing the animals to act crazy, or "loco." Horses that eat locoweed may start to stagger and fall over.

Poison hemlock

Poison hemlock *(Conium maculatum).* Poison hemlock has tiny white flowers in umbrella-shaped masses. The tall stem of a poison hemlock plant has feathery leaves that can each be over a foot in length. The plant grows in moist pastures in almost every state. It can kill livestock that eat it.

AGRONOMY

Meadow death camas *(Zigadenus venenosus)*. Found in the forests, foothills, and meadows of the western United States, meadow death camas has small, white, star-shaped flowers with six petals. The plant has narrow leaves rising from its base. All parts of the meadow death camas are poisonous, including the leaves, stem, pollen, bulb, and flowers. Grazing animals—including sheep, cattle, and horses—can become ill or die from consuming large quantities of this plant.

Leafy spurge *(Euphorbia esula)*. Leafy spurge can grow up to 3 feet tall, with small yellowish-green leaves surrounding the flowers. The root of the leafy spurge can extend more than 20 feet into the ground. Livestock can die from eating this plant in large amounts.

Common milkweed *(Asclepias syriaca)*. Common milkweed is found in the central and eastern United States, where it grows in cultivated fields, sunny dry pastures, and roadside ditches. The crown-shaped pale purple flowers grow in clusters, and the large oval-shaped leaves are covered with hairs. The leaves and sap of this plant are poisonous and bitter-tasting to livestock, and sheep can die after eating large amounts of milkweed.

PLANT SCIENCE

Agronomy

Ladybird beetle

Control of Insect Pests, Plant Diseases, and Weeds in Field Crops

Traditional pesticides and herbicides contain toxic chemicals that can kill beneficial wildlife and leave a chemical residue on plants. Equally effective—and environmentally friendly—pest- and weed-control options are now available to farmers and ranchers. A few of these innovations include:

Biological Controls

This approach involves introducing predators, parasites, or forms of life such as bacteria that will destroy invasive weeds and insect pests. Among the earliest and most successful examples of this form of control occurred in the 1880s. The California citrus crop was being wiped out by an insect called the cottony cushion scale. The citrus growers imported the Vedalia ladybird beetle from Australia to eat the cottony cushion scale, and within two years the pest was controlled.

> **Extremely small:** The tiny seeds of some orchids are smaller than some bacteria. An ounce of orchid seeds can contain more than 35 million individual seeds.

Cultural Controls

Farmers can change their normal farming routines so that they interfere with the life cycles and feeding habits of harmful insects. Some farmers plant more than one crop at a time in their fields. Because many varieties of insects depend on one kind of plant for their entire food supply, if farmers mix their plantings then insects may not have enough to eat, and the insect population will stay at a tolerable level.

Fall Cultivation

Soil cultivation in the fall destroys weed seeds and insect larvae and pupae buried in the earth by crushing them or exposing them to the surface cold.

Integrated Pest Management

Chemical pesticides have been used extensively in farming, but many pesticides have a negative environmental impact, killing beneficial insects and plants. They also may persist for a long time in nature, creating danger to people and wildlife. In fact, a number of pesticides have been banned. Because of the concerns about pesticides, some farmers use a combination approach called integrated pest management (IPM) to naturally control insects and weeds. IPM uses all suitable pest-control techniques in combinations that are environmentally sound and compatible with local conditions. IPM techniques include monitoring the insect or plant pest, using biological and cultural control methods, and resorting to chemical controls only when no other effective method is available.

AGRONOMY

Harvesting, Storing, and Processing Field Crops

Simply growing a bountiful crop is not the end of a farmer's work. The crop must be harvested. Every field crop requires a different method of harvest. For example, corn is usually harvested with a combine machine. The combine machine first picks the ears of corn off of the cornstalks. The ears of corn are then shucked, which means the husks surrounding the ear are removed. Then the corn kernels are shelled, or removed from the corncob. The combine machine then dumps the shelled corn into a waiting truck or wagon. All these harvesting steps are accomplished by the combine machine during the harvest. Different harvesting methods are used for wheat, barley, rice, and other crops.

Once the crop has been harvested, it is transported to a storage area such as a grain elevator, or sold directly to a processor. Ask your merit badge counselor or extension agent where local field crops are sent after harvesting, and arrange to visit these storage or processing operations.

Extremely fast-growing: Certain species of bamboo can grow more than 3 feet in a single day.

52   PLANT SCIENCE

Horticulture

The branch of plant science known as horticulture covers the practice of growing fruits, vegetables, nuts, flowers, and ornamental plants in small gardens or orchards. A horticulturalist could be a scientist studying how to eliminate plant diseases in a community vegetable garden, a farmer raising fruits and nuts in a commercial orchard, or a winemaker growing grapes in a vineyard.

Hardiness Zones

Before horticulturalists plant gardens or trees, they need to identify their climate zone. Plants are adapted to specific climates. For example, a plant that grows well in the arid deserts of the southwestern United States might quickly die if planted in the cool, rainy climate of the Pacific Northwest.

Fortunately, there is an easy way to figure out what plants grow in your area. The U.S. Department of Agriculture has produced a hardiness zone map, a quick visual guide that helps you know what plants will grow in different climates. The hardiness zone map is divided into 11 zones; Zone 1 is the coldest and Zone 11 is the warmest. Each zone represents a 10-degree difference in average minimum temperature.

> You can access a more detailed map of U.S. agricultural regions on the USDA National Arboretum website: http://www.usna.usda.gov/Hardzone/ushzmap.html.
> Use the map to locate your town and region.

HORTICULTURE

Here's an example of how the hardiness zones are arranged. Zone 5, which includes Des Moines, Iowa, has minimum winter temperatures between -10 to -20 degrees. Zone 6, which is farther south than Zone 5, has minimum temperatures between 0 and -10 degrees. Zone 6 includes the city of St. Louis, Missouri. Colder zones are usually found farther north and at higher elevations. Warmer zones are found farther south and at lower elevations.

Factors other than the minimum temperature of the hardiness zones also can influence which plants are suitable for your area. Some of these factors include yearly rainfall, wind conditions, soil types, and daytime temperatures.

The table shows a few plant species that are adapted for each hardiness zone. To find more plants that you can grow successfully in your hardiness zone, visit a local nursery or check gardening reference books.

Agricultural Zones for the United States

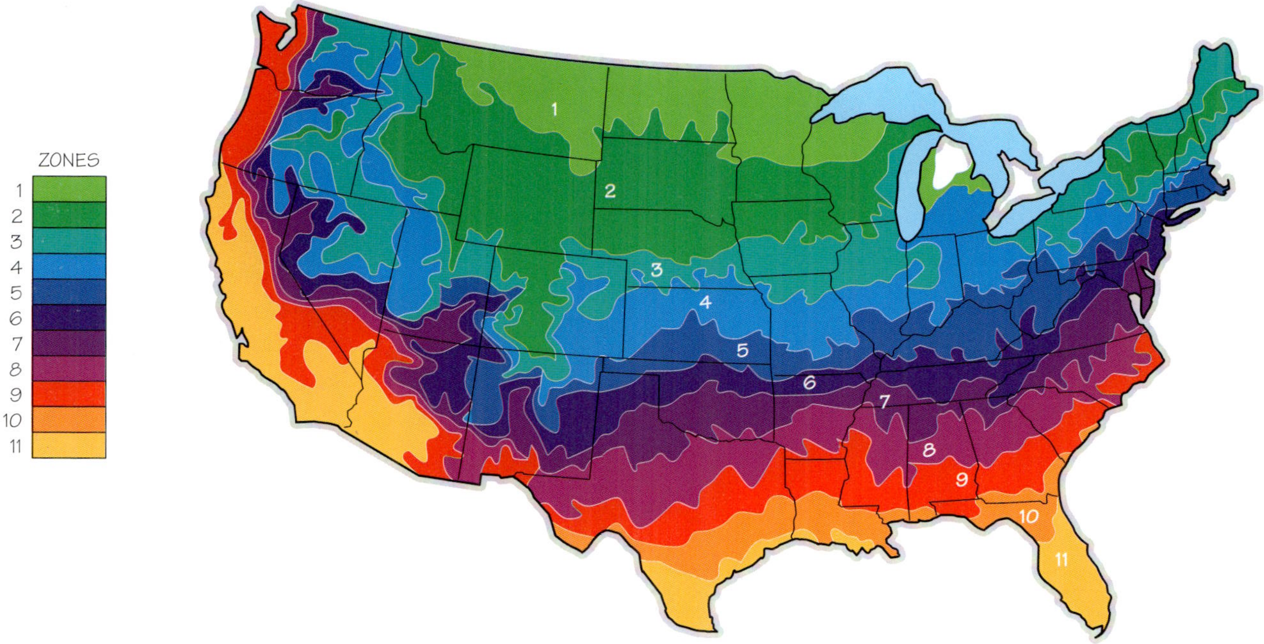

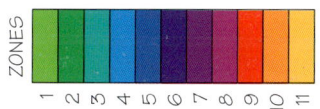

HORTICULTURE

Hardiness Zones and Suggested Plants for the United States*

**USDA Zone,
Low Temperature,
Example Cities** — **Plant by Botanical Name (and Common Name)**

Zone

Below -50 degrees F
Fairbanks, Alaska

Betula glandulosa (Dwarf birch)
Empetrum nigrum (Crowberry)
Populus fremuloides (Quaking aspen)
Potentilla pensylvanica (Pennsylvania cinquefoil)
Rhododendron lapponicum (Lapland rhododendron)
Salix reticulate (Netleaf willow)

Zone

-50 to -40 degrees F
Prudhoe Bay, Alaska
Unalakleet, Alaska
Pinecreek, Minn.

Arctostaphylos uva-ursi (Bearberry)
Betula papyrifera (Paper birch)
Cornus canadensis (Bunchberry dogwood)
Elaeagnus commutata (Silverberry)
Larix laricina (Eastern larch)
Potentilla fruticosa (Bush cinquefoil)
Ulmus americana (American elm)
Viburnum trilobum (American cranberry bush)

Zone

-40 to -30 degrees F
International Falls, Minn.
St. Michael, Alaska
Tomahawk, Wis.
Sidney, Mont.

Berberis thunbetgii (Japanese bayberry)
Betula pendula (European white birch)
Cornus alba (Tatarian dogwood)
Elaeagnus angustifolia (Russian olive)
Junipercus communes (Common juniper)
Lonicera tatarica (Tatarian honeysuckle)
Malus baocata (Siberian crabapple)
Rhododendron southern Indian hybrids (Indian azalea)
Syringa vulgaris (Common lilac)
Thuia occidentalis (American arborvitae)

*This information was taken from the USDA website.

HORTICULTURE

Zone

-30 to -20 degrees
Minneapolis/
St. Paul, Minn.
Lewistown, Mont.
Northwood, Iowa
Omaha, Neb.

Acer saccharum (Sugar maple)
Acer platanoides (Norway maple)
Aristolochia durior (Dutchman's pipe)
Forsythia ovata (Early forsythia)
Hydrangea paniculata (Panicle hydrangea)
Juniperus chinensis (Chinese juniper)
Ligustrum amurense (Amur river privet)
Parthenocissus quinquefolia (Virginia creeper)
Spiraea x vanhouttei (Vanhouffe spirea)

Zone

-20 to -10 degrees F
Des Moines, Iowa
Chicago, Ill.
Columbia, Mo.
Mansfield, Penn.

Cornus florida (Flowering dogwood)
Deutzia gracilis (Slender deutzia)
Forsythia suspensa (Weeping forsythia)
Ginkgo biloba (Ginkgo, Maidenhair tree)
Hibiscus syriacus (Shrub althea)
Iberis sempervirens (Evergreen candytuft)
Lagerstroemia indica (Crape myrtle)
Ligustrum vulgare (Common privet)
Mahonia aquitolium (Oregon hollygrape)
Metasequoia glyptostroboides
(Dawn redwood)
Rhododendron "America" (Hybrid rhododendron)
Paithenocissus tricuspidata (Boston ivy)
Rosa multiflora (Japanese rose)
Taxus cuspidata (Japanese yew)
Viburnum burkwoodii (Burkwood viburnum)

Zone

-10 to 0 degrees F
St. Louis, Mo.
Lebanon, Penn.
McMinnville, Tenn.
Branson, Mo.

Acer palmatum (Japanese maple)
Buxus sempervirens (Common boxwood)
Cercis chinensis (Chinese redbud)
Chamaecyparis lawsoniana (Lawson cypress)
Cytisus x praecox (Warminster broom)
Euonymus follunei (Winter creeper)
Hedera helix (English ivy)
Ilex opaca (American holly)
Ligustrum ovalifolium (California privet)
Pieris japonica (Japanese andromeda)
Prunus yedoensis (Yoshino cherry)

Zone 7
0 to 10 degrees F
Oklahoma City, Okla.
South Boston, Va.
Little Rock, Ark.
Griffin, Ga.

Acer macrophylium (Bigleaf maple)
Rhododendron Kurume hybrids (Kurume azalea)
Cedrus atlantica (Atlas cedar)
Cotoneaster microphylla (Small-leaf cotoneaster)
Ilex aquifolium (English holly)
Taxus baccata (English yew)

Zone 8
10 to 20 degrees F
Tifton, Ga.
Dallas, Texas
Austin, Texas

Pistacia chinensis (Chinese pistachio)
Lagerstroemia (Crepe myrtle)
Ilex vomitoria (Yaupon holly)
Cuphea hyssopifolia (Mexican heather)
Buxus japonica (Japanese boxwood)

Zone 9
20 to 30 degrees F
Houston, Texas
St. Augustine, Fla.
Brownsville, Texas
Fort Pierce, Fla.

Asparagus setacous (Asparagus fern)
Eucalyptus globulus (Tasmanian blue gum)
Syzygium paniculatum (Australian bush cherry)
Fuchsia hybrids (Fuchsia)
Grevillea robusta (Silk oak)
Schinus molle (California pepper tree)

Zone 10
30 to 40 degrees F
Naples, Fla.
Victorville, Calif.
Miami, Fla.
Phoenix, Ariz.

Bougainvillea spectabilis (Bougainvillea)
Cassia fistula (Golden shower)
Eucalyptus citriodora (Lemon eucalyptus)
Ficus elastica (Rubber plant)
Ensete ventricosum (Ensete)
Roystonea regia (Royal palm)

Zone 11
Above 40 degrees F
Honolulu, Hawaii

Bougainvillea spectabilis (Bougainvillea)
Cassia fistula (Golden shower)
Eucalyptus citriodora (Lemon eucalyptus)
Ficus elastica (Rubber plant)
Ensete ventricosum (Ensete)
Roystonea regia (Royal palm)

Landscape Design

Horticulturalists often use trees, flowers, and other plants to design landscapes. Landscape design refers to the planning of the look of land not covered by buildings or roads. Landscape designers create outdoor spaces that are more pleasing to look at and are safer and healthier than they would have been without a planned design.

A landscape design changes as plants and trees grow, flower, and eventually die. A landscape designer selects trees, shrubs, and ground covers that will thrive in particular soil and climate conditions. They choose plants for their unique characteristics and contributions to the design plan.

In landscape design, scale is the relationship of the design to the people who will use it. A person senses when the scale feels too large, too small, or just right.

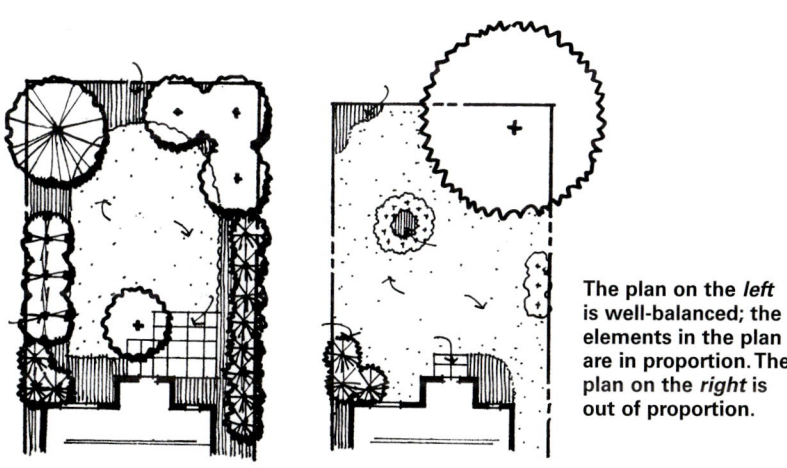

The plan on the *left* is well-balanced; the elements in the plan are in proportion. The plan on the *right* is out of proportion.

Landscape designers and landscape architects (professionals who create outdoor places that people care about and want to visit) use a concept called *xeriscape* (pronounced *ZEER-i-skape*) when planning a landscape. This means they minimize areas of turf (grass), improve the soil, and utilize indigenous (native) and drought-tolerant plants. This saves water, money, and time because it takes less water (and watering time) to keep such an area thriving.

HORTICULTURE

Some Common Horticultural Terms and Definitions

Annuals. Annual flowers and plants grow for one season and then die. They usually grow and bloom during spring, summer, or fall, dying after the first frost of winter. New annuals must be planted every year.

Perennials. Perennial plants come back year after year without replanting. Many perennial plants lose their leaves and die back in the fall or after the first frost. When the weather warms up, perennial plants grow back again. They often increase in size over the years.

Shade tolerance. A plant's shade tolerance describes how well it grows in shade. Shade tolerance varies quite a bit. Many plants require full sun to thrive, while others can tolerate half a day or more of shade. Some plants, such as ferns, do fine in full shade.

Moisture requirement. All plants need water, but the amount they need—their moisture requirement—varies. For example, blue flag iris does best in the damp soil along the margins of ponds. Other plants, including some native and ornamental grasses, are drought tolerant.

Mulch. A layer of material such as organic compost, bark chips, straw, or black plastic is placed on the surface of the soil. Mulch raises the temperature of the soil, reduces weed growth, and helps hold in moisture.

Propagation. Plant reproduction occurs either through seeds (sexual reproduction) or through vegetative (asexual reproduction) techniques like grafting.

Pruning. Plant parts like stems or branches are removed to increase the plant's beauty, to remove dead material, and to reduce crowding of the remaining living branches. Pruning also eliminates excess living plant material that drains energy away from the production of fruits and flowers.

Cultivar. A cultivar is a CULTIvated VARiety of a plant that has been selected by horticulturalists for certain traits (such as unique taste and color in apples). Cultivar traits are propagated through grafting, not through sexual reproduction.

> **Deadheading.** Removing dead flowers and seeds from a plant after they have bloomed is called deadheading. Deadheading can cause plants to produce a second set of blooms once the first flower heads have been removed. Rose plants, for example, often produce blooms throughout the summer and fall if they are deadheaded.

Landscape designers consider plant size, form, texture, and color, and then apply basic design principles to planting arrangements. The ultimate sizes of trees, shrubs, flowers, and ground cover are important landscape design considerations. If you plant a tree in a small space that it eventually outgrows, you may have to spend a lot of time and money removing that tree from the landscape. Landscape designers must consider whether the plants in any design grow slowly or quickly. For example, a fast-growing tree, such as a Lombardy poplar, could be a good choice for an area where you need to grow a windbreak to shelter a house from the wind.

Plants that grow more slowly, such as a dense evergreen tree, might be considered in areas where the landscape designer wants to create deep shade in a few years. Another consideration is texture, which is determined by the characteristics of a plant's various parts. For example, plant leaves may be shiny, prickly, fuzzy, large, small, broad, or narrow. The textures of the plants chosen for a landscape add to the overall effect.

Stem Grafting

As discussed earlier, plants can propagate, or reproduce, in several ways—from seeds, tubers, roots, and cuttings. Another important propagation method is grafting. Stem grafting involves attaching a small upper branch called a *scion,* or bud stock, to a lower branch or trunk called the *rootstock.*

The method of joining two plants together has many advantages in horticulture. Some plant varieties cannot be propagated from seeds, so grafting is the only method available. Plant varieties also can be grown in different areas of the country by grafting the cultivar onto a rootstock that is more adapted to the local climate. Plants that are often grafted include grapevines, as well as a variety of fruit and nut trees such as cherry, peach, apple, and pecans.

Horticulture

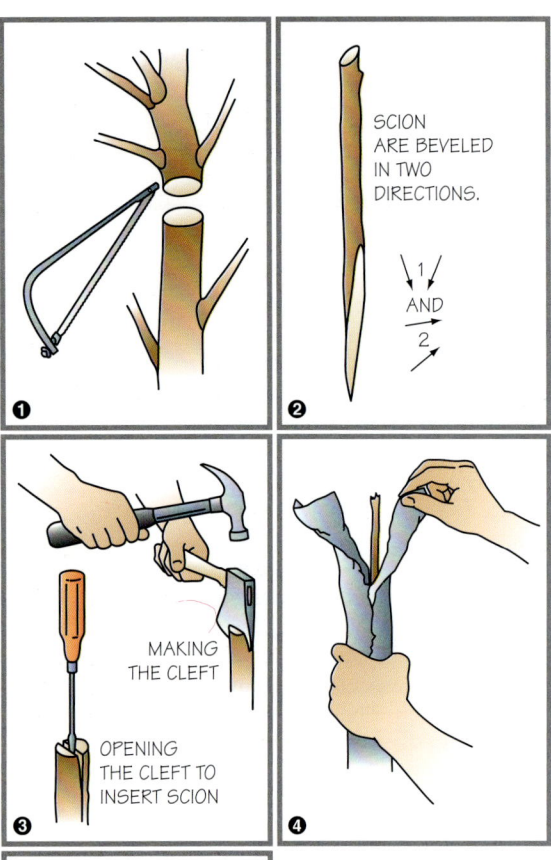

Grafting is usually done in spring, just prior to the start of the growing season. Here's the procedure:

Step 1—Use trunks 1 1/2 to 3 1/2 inches in diameter for rootstock. Cut straight across the trunk with a sharp saw.

Step 2—The scion should be the same species as the rootstock. Cut off 3 to 4 inches of a branch with three or four buds. Taper the ends of the scion.

Step 3— Use a small hand ax and hammer to make a cleft in the rootstock. Spread the split in the rootstock and insert the scion pieces. The *cambium* layer of both rootstock and scion must be in close contact. (The cambium is the soft tissue between the wood and the bark.)

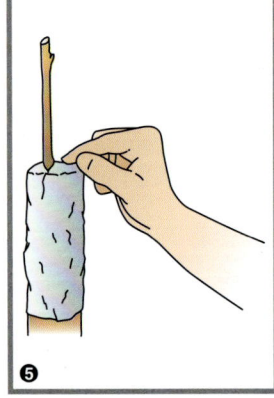

Step 4—Cut an 8- to 12-inch square of aluminum foil. Wrap the foil around the rootstock. Tear or cut a line down the center of the square as shown.

Step 5—Fold each side of the divided end of the foil around the graft. Cover all cut surfaces.

HORTICULTURE

Step 6—Cut off one corner of a small plastic bag. Slip the bag over the graft and work the graft through the hole at the corner. Pull the bag down gently.

Step 7—Tie the bag at the cut corner around the graft using a rubber band, budding strip, raffia, or polyethylene tape.

Step 8—Tie the lower end of the bag around the stock. Use tape or a large rubber budding strip to secure the lower end of the bag.

Step 9—Coat the cut surface of the tip end of the graft with grafting wax.

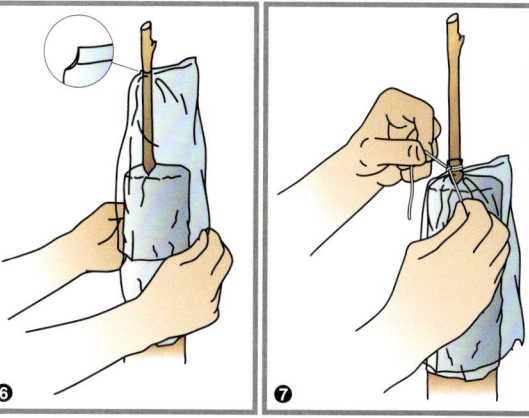
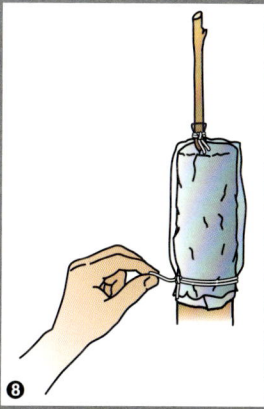
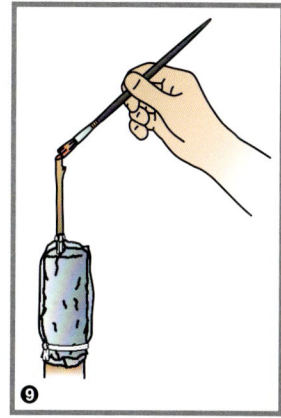

Bedding Plants

Bedding plants can be propagated from cuttings or from seeds grown indoors, then transferred outside after they have produced a few leaves. You can start bedding plants indoors by planting seeds in potting soil. Once the seedlings sprout, put them under bright lights and fertilize them with a liquid fertilizer. Bedding plants grow best in well-lighted areas. You also will need to give them plenty of water.

About a week before you are ready to transfer your bedding plants outdoors, you should *harden off* the plants. This means you should gradually reduce the amount of water and fertilizer the plants receive and put them outside for a few hours each day to expose them to cooler air and drier conditions. This helps the seedlings adjust to the harsher climate before you transplant them outside.

Fruit, Berry, and Nut Crops

If you choose to plant an orchard, you must plan it carefully. Although you must take full care of the trees for just one season in order to meet this requirement, the trees may live for 30 or more years.

Certain factors are critical to the success of your planting:

- **Location**—Most fruit and nut trees require full sunlight for peak productivity.
- **Air circulation**—Wind movement away from the trees reduces the risk of frost damage.

- **Water drainage**—Soil should be well-drained, with no seepage places or wet spots.
- **Soil fertility**—Fruit trees need deep, rich soil with the same essential elements required by other crops.
- **Spacing**—Trees must be planted according to their expected size at maturation.

Some fruit crops (such as cherries, grapes, and peaches) can pollinate themselves, but many do not produce pollen or are sterile to their own pollen (such as blueberries and apples). In order to produce fruit (or nuts or berries), the sterile plants depend on cross-pollination and fertilization from a second plant of a different variety that will bloom at the same time and produce pollen. Get advice from an expert about choosing plants for your fruit, berry, or nut crop.

The Dirt on Potting Soil Mixes

Manufactured potting mixes differ in quality, price, and ingredients, but none contains real soil. Garden dirt has bacteria, insects, and weed seeds, but commercially prepared potting soil mixes are sterile and can be used straight from the bag.

To grow healthy plants, use a good quality potting mix that:

- Is dense enough to support the plants.
- Allows air and water to pass through, yet holds adequate moisture.
- Retains nutrients and slow-release fertilizers.

Most potting mixes combine organic matter (such as peat moss or ground pine bark) and inorganic material (such as washed sand, perlite, or vermiculite). The ingredients (and their textures) affect the characteristics of the mix. For example, vermiculite increases water retention; perlite speeds up water drainage.

The potting mix you choose will depend on how you plan to use it. Plants grown from seeds require very light mixes that are full of air—otherwise the seedlings will die in heavy, wet potting soil. Cuttings, on the other hand, require a dense mix that will hold them up.

HORTICULTURE

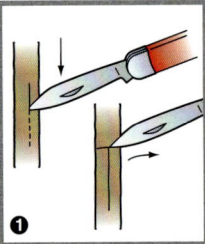

Bud Grafting

Many growers try to improve the quality of their trees by grafting a desired variety onto a strong rootstock. They may wish to encourage dwarfing in a high-density orchard, provide a strong trunk for a different variety, or induce cold tolerance or disease resistance. Fruit trees often are propagated by this method.

Budding involves grafting a dormant side bud onto rootstock during the growing season, usually in July or August after new growth has stopped. Follow these steps for the grafting technique known as T or shield budding:

Step 1—Make a T cut to bark depth on one-year-old rootstock.

Step 2—Cut a bud from this year's growth on a mature healthy scion. The cutting should be shield-shaped, with part of the leaf stem intact for a handle.

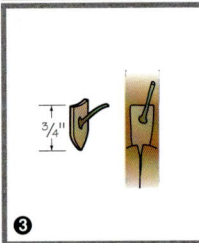

Step 3—Carefully slip the shield with the bud into the T cut.

Step 4—Press the shield down snugly.

Step 5—Hold the bark flaps tightly against the bud and wrap them securely in place with polyethylene budding tape or rubber budding strips, which break down by weathering.

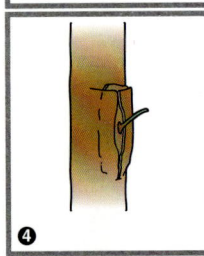

Step 6—The next spring, when the bud begins to grow, remove the wrapping and prune the rootstock 6 to 8 inches above the bud. Use the rootstock as a stake to tie the new shoot.

Step 7—At the end of the first growing season, cut off the rootstock just above the new shoot.

Step 8—Eventually, the new shoot will grow straight.

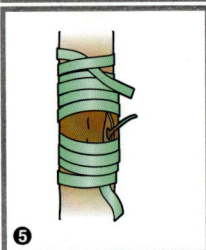   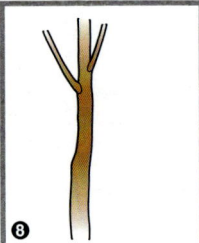

Fresh to Processed

How long will you have to wait to pick your fruit, berries, or nuts? Various fruit crops require different amounts of time to produce their first good harvest. You can pick strawberries in one year, but you will have to wait six to 10 years to collect pecans.

Fruit crops can be consumed as fresh or processed foods. For example, nuts are often processed for butters and oils. Fruits may be cut up and canned or frozen, or processed for jams and pie fillings. Berries, too, are canned or frozen, or turned into syrup, juice, or wine.

Woody Ornamental Plants

Woody ornamentals are trees and shrubs that people grow because of their attractive features. Three major types of ornamental trees — coniferous, evergreen, and deciduous — produce a variety of growth forms, shapes, and sizes. Shrubs are smaller than trees, but larger and stronger than flowers or vegetables. The characteristic form or manner of growth of a shrub or tree is referred to as its *habit*. For example, evergreen habits might include an upright evergreen shrub, a compact evergreen hedge, or a sprawling evergreen bush.

Coniferous trees produce cones containing seeds. Examples are pine, cedar, and fir trees. Most conifers are also evergreens.

HORTICULTURE

Evergreen trees and shrubs keep their green leaves year-round. Examples are palms, citrus, many kinds of rhododendrons, and some magnolias.

Deciduous trees lose all of their leaves at one time each year, usually in the fall or early winter. Examples are dogwood, oak, and pecan trees.

HORTICULTURE

Planting Your Own Trees or Shrubs

Planting trees and shrubs helps beautify an area and hold the soil in place. Trees and shrubs also provide shade, shelter, and food for wildlife. You need to consider many factors before planting trees and shrubs, including your soil type, how long the tree will likely live, the hardiness zone you live in, the size and shape of the tree or shrub when fully grown, and the care the tree or shrub will require as it grows. Because there are so many things to consider before you plant a tree or shrub, it is a good idea to consult gardening books, your merit badge counselor, or a county extension agent for advice.

Once you get the tree or shrub you will plant, be sure to keep it well-watered until you plant it. Dig planting holes spaced according to the recommendations for the kind of tree or shrub you are planting. It is important that the holes you dig are large enough to hold all the roots without crowding them. Be sure the soil at the bottom of the hole is not packed so hard that it will interfere with root growth. If the soil is dry, you might need to put a little water in the hole. Press the soil carefully and extra firmly about the roots as you fill the hole, because air pockets in the root zone could kill the tree or shrub seedling. Stake the tree, if necessary, and take care not to damage the trunk or branches.

Prevent weeds, grass, and other plants from competing with the newly planted shrub or tree. A layer of mulch will help keep weeds down. See that the tree or shrub gets regular water either from rain or from watering. During its first year, the tree or shrub needs pruning to train it into a strong, well-shaped plant. In later years, pruning is done to remove dead, diseased, or damaged branches, or to redirect growth.

PLANT SCIENCE 71

Pruning Techniques

Like people, plants require discipline and training. Good pruning directs growth and eliminates bad habits and problems. If you understand the relationship between the location of the buds on a branch and the position of the pruning cuts, you can train a plant to grow as you wish. Poor pruning results in an unruly plant.

Terminal buds—at the ends of stems and branches—produce a hormone that encourages most of the growth to occur at the tips of the plant. Lateral (side) buds on a branch do not develop well as long as the terminal bud is in place. If you prune the terminal bud, the lateral buds will grow side shoots. To encourage horizontal growth, select an outward-facing bud and cut the branch at an angle directly above the bud. For vertical growth, cut the branch at an angle directly above an inward-facing bud.

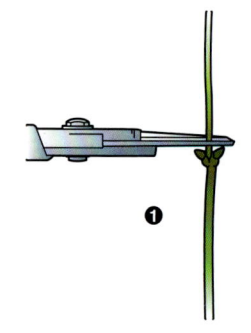

1. Pruning to opposite buds. Cut squarely across the stem above a pair of buds (as close as you can without touching or damaging them). A pair of side shoots will then grow.

2. Pruning for horizontal growth. Make an angled cut directly above an outward-facing bud.

3. Pruning for vertical growth. Make an angled cut directly above an inward-facing bud.

You should prune at different times of the year depending on which type of plant you have. The best time to prune spring-flowering shrubs and vines is in the spring, after they have flowered. The best time for shade trees is in the midwinter dormant season.

HORTICULTURE

Use the right kind of pruning tools for the task, and keep them sharpened and maintained to make clean cuts.

- **Hand shears** for twigs less than 1/2 inch in diameter
- **Lopping shears** for branches 1/2 to 1 inch in diameter
- **Pruning saw** for limbs more than 1 inch in diameter
- **Hedge shears** for formal pruning and shaping
- **Electric hedge shears** for faster pruning and shaping

Prune a hedge so the base of the hedge is broader than the top. This shape will allow sunlight to reach all the foliage.

PLANT SCIENCE

Trees, the Environment, and Humans

Trees are one of the largest plants on Earth and also one of the most important. In addition to providing us with fruit, nuts, and wood, trees benefit us and Earth in the following ways:

- **By protecting and nurturing the soil**—The roots of trees hold the soil together, reducing soil erosion. When the leaves, branches, and other parts of a tree die and fall to the ground, they decompose and enrich the soil.

- **By reducing energy use**—Trees planted around a house provide protection from cold winter winds as well as hot sunshine, which reduces the need to use energy for heating and air-conditioning. The air-conditioning energy costs for a house can be reduced by as much as half by simply planting several shade trees near the house.

- **By reducing air pollution**—Carbon dioxide is a gas emitted by the burning of fossil fuels. Scientists believe that the amount of carbon dioxide gas is increasing in the atmosphere, which may contribute to an accelerated warming of the planet. Trees can help reduce the amount of carbon dioxide in the air, because they absorb carbon dioxide during photosynthesis.

- **By providing habitats**—Both living and dead trees are home to thousands of species of other plants, birds, insects, and mammals, including rare and endangered species.

- **By creating livable communities**—Trees planted in urban areas provide privacy around homes, reduce the sound of traffic, and create an oasis of quiet and calm in city parks.

Horticulture

Home Gardening

Growing a garden can provide you with beautiful flowers as well as food. There are many fruits and vegetables you can grow in a garden. Plants that grow best in cooler weather include broccoli, Brussels sprouts, cabbage, celery, collards, kale, lettuce, okra, peas, potatoes, and spinach. Other fruits and vegetables grow better in warmer weather, including beans, blackberries, cantaloupe, carrots, corn, cucumber, peppers, squash, tomatoes, and watermelon. Consult gardening books, your merit badge counselor, or your county extension agent for more information on which vegetables and flowers would grow best in your garden. Also find out how and when to plant your garden and the pests and weeds you may encounter during the growing season.

Steps to Prepare the Soil

Step 1—For a new bed, use a hoe or square-bladed shovel to remove all existing plant material.

Step 2—Turn the soil with a spade or tiller, working the topsoil to a depth of 8 or more inches. Continue turning the soil until the particles are no larger than golf balls. Remove rocks, roots, and other debris. Rake the ground level.

Step 3—Cover the ground with a 3- or 4-inch layer of organic matter (manure, compost, peat moss) to improve the soil. For clay soil, add 1 or 2 inches of washed brick sand. With a spade or spading fork, turn the new material into the soil as before.

Step 4—Rake the ground again.

Step 5—Treat the bed with a fumigant to eliminate soil-borne insects, diseases, and weeds. Read and follow the directions carefully. Check with your merit badge counselor or parent before you fumigate because misuse may be harmful to your health.

Horticulture

Planning and Soil Preparation

Plan the location of your garden. Using paper and pencil, map your plantings. Decide what you need to do to prepare your plot.

Planting Your Garden

To thrive, flowers and vegetables must be spaced appropriately and planted at the depth recommended for the particular plants. Dig holes slightly larger than the diameter of the plant. Water both the soil and the plants before setting them into the ground. Spread the roots out, then sprinkle soil into the hole to the level of the bed. Water in heavily to eliminate air pockets around the roots. Add a layer of mulch around the plants to control weeds, conserve moisture, and keep the soil cool.

Certain plants need extra support to stand straight. Set metal, wood, or bamboo stakes next to the plant and tie the stem to the stake with old nylon stockings or strips of cloth to avoid damaging the plant. Certain vines may be staked to trellises. Many gardeners use wire cages to support tomato plants. Try to stake the flower or vegetable when you set the plant in the garden to avoid damaging the root system when you push the stake into the ground.

Chemical fertilizers are toxic and dangerous, just like pesticides and fungicides. When using fertilizers, be sure to read and follow the manufacturer's instructions. Use these chemicals only under close adult supervision.

Feeding Your Garden

Your garden plot needs nutrients to help the plants thrive. Fertilizing your garden may be necessary to promote better plant growth. Dry fertilizers are often used to cover a large area such as a lawn or a large garden. Liquid fertilizers are mixed with water and are poured or sprayed onto foliage or around the plant's base. Liquid fertilizers work well for small garden plots.

- General fertilizers contain all of the primary plant nutrients—nitrogen (for healthy foliage), phosphorus (for developing a strong root system), and potassium (the "energy booster"). Such fertilizers use a numbering system (such as "12-4-8") to measure these nutrients. The higher the number, the more nutrient in the fertilizer. The first number measures nitrogen; the second, phosphorus; the third, potassium. The types of plants and soil you have will help you determine which fertilizer to use.

- Special-purpose fertilizers contain nutrients for a particular kind of plant. You might see fertilizers labeled "African violet food" or "camellia food." These fertilizers are specially mixed with the balance of nutrients these plants need most.

HORTICULTURE

- Simple fertilizers contain only one of the primary nutrients.
- Natural fertilizers are made from the decayed remains of living organisms. Blood meal, animal manure, compost from yard or garden waste, and worm castings are examples of natural fertilizers.

Caring for Your Garden Throughout the Season

Check your plants often. Pull weeds. Look for damage caused by insects or disease, and treat appropriately. Are the leaves wilted or yellow? Make sure the plants are getting the right amount of water. You can encourage more blooms if you deadhead any faded flowers.

To make a plant grow bushier and more compact, pinch back the center shoot with your fingertips or scissors. That will encourage side shoots to grow. Prune the plant (only if necessary) to direct growth or remove damaged parts. The best time to prune varies according to the type of plant, so check before you cut.

Many gardeners prefer to use alternatives to chemical fertilizers. Composting (recycling grass clippings, leaves, raw kitchen waste) and biological controls (using living creatures such as ladybugs to control insects and plant diseases) are two popular methods.

Keeping Wildlife in Mind

Planting a garden or designing a landscape gives you the opportunity to improve wildlife habitats. Here are some ideas:

- Plant native flowers that attract birds and butterflies. Your local extension agent or merit badge counselor can help you choose suitable plants for your area. Also check native plant books to find species that are beneficial to the wildlife in your area.

- Install birdhouses, bird feeders, and birdbaths. Use different types of food (sunflower seeds, suet, thistle seed) to attract different species of birds.

- Leave trees and shrubs unpruned to provide more branches and hiding places for birds and small mammals.

- Place tree logs on the ground to provide perching places for birds and small animals. As the logs rot, birds and animals may burrow into the wood looking for insects.

Field Botany

Plant scientists who study plants in their natural environment are called field botanists. These specialists are expert at identifying wild plants, describing the location and types of plant communities, and observing the impact over time of climate, animal, and human changes on plant diversity.

Field botanists study plants in their natural environment and bring plant specimens back to laboratories for further study. By collecting, pressing, and identifying plants, field botanists help gather data on plant populations and locations—information that can then be used in later research.

Observing Nature—The Essential Skill of Field Botanists

Field botanists pay much closer attention to plants than most people. You can learn many of the skills of field botanists by becoming more aware of what is growing around you. Begin by noticing the sizes and shapes of the trees at a park, forest, or other natural area near your home. Note how close together they are growing and which species are the largest or most abundant. Which plants grow well in the shade? Which grow in the sun? Is there evidence of fire, disease, or strong winds? Study the network of fine lines crisscrossing the surface of a leaf. Search the ground for fruit, seed pods, or nuts, and break one open. Take a plant identification book with you, and read about a plant's uses, range, longevity, and special characteristics.

It is illegal to take plant specimens from national parks in the United States. If you want to collect in a state or county park or national forest, always get permission from a park ranger or custodian.

Extremely smelly: The giant titan arum gives off the smell of rotting flesh. This terrible smell attracts flies and other insects that pollinate the flower.

FIELD BOTANY

The following questions can help you begin your field exploration:
- How is the plant similar to and different from nearby plants?
- How are the leaves or needles shaped?
- Does the plant bear flowers or fruiting bodies?
- What kind of soil is it growing in—wet, dry, sand, gravel, black dirt?
- What does the landscape near the plant look like?
- How do climate and latitude influence the plants?
- How is the plant affecting the environment around it?

Tips for Collecting Plants

- Always ask permission before taking a plant specimen from private property.
- Take a notebook and a pen or pencil. Record as much information as possible about the location where you found each plant.
- Take several plastic bags with you on your plant collecting trips. If you do not have time to put each plant into a plant press when you collect it, you can store it in a labeled, sealed plastic bag to keep it fresh until you get home.
- Use a pair of plant shears or sharp scissors to cut the pieces of a large plant specimen from the main plant. You will cause less damage to the remaining plant than if you break off a leaf or stem.
- Wear gloves when collecting plant specimens with prickly stems.
- Some plants are dangerous to collect. In many parts of North America, you may encounter poison ivy, poison oak, or stinging nettles. If you touch the leaves of any of these three plants, your skin may itch and blister. If you come in contact with one of these plants, thoroughly wash the area with soap and water. Apply hydrocortisone cream for itching if needed. Learn how to identify these three plants, and avoid them.

Pressing Plant Specimens

Placing plant specimens in a plant press forces them to dry without shriveling. The dried plant specimens can then be mounted on a sheet of paper and used in the future for identification and comparison to other similar plants. Properly pressed plant specimens have been stored for hundreds of years without losing their identifying shapes.

Use old newspapers to make a press. Place the specimens in it carefully, so they dry flat and are not creased. Arrange them in a lifelike position to show their parts to best advantage. When the specimens are thoroughly dry, mount them in a notebook or on cardstock. Transparent glue or small strips of gummed cloth are preferred for affixing specimens. For this requirement, however, you may use double-sided tape to mount the specimens—but it is not recommended for a permanent collection. Label each with the common name of the specimen, the scientific name (genus and species), the date, and the place it was collected.

A homemade press is suitable to dry and flatten plant specimens before mounting. After mounting, keep the specimens under pressure so they will not curl or break.

Voucher Specimens

Field botanists often find plants in areas where they previously were not known. Sometimes they find new plant species never before identified by scientists. In such cases, botanists often collect and preserve these plants as voucher specimens. A voucher specimen is a plant sample that is collected and stored for future study or comparison with other plant samples from other areas—and from other years or even centuries. It is important because it provides physical evidence that a plant species existed in a specific location. Voucher specimens document the occurrence of rare plants and indicate the geographic spread of invasive plant species.

Field Botany

Using a Plant Key

Among the useful tools for identifying plants are plant keys, available both as books and as interactive websites. A plant key guides you step-by-step to the identity of a plant species. Each plant key addresses particular kinds of vegetation (trees, for example) and may be further focused on a specific region (such as North America).

Plant keys are typically constructed with an either/or format, asking you to make a series of yes-or-no decisions that will steadily narrow your choices until you come upon the specific description of the plant you want to identify. A typical sequence might lead you this way:

Needlelike leaves or broad-leaf leaves? If broad-leaf, then . . .

Compound leaves or simple leaves? If compound, then . . .

Thorns or spines present, or thorns or spines absent? If thorns or spines absent, then . . .

Leaves smooth, toothed, or lobed? If lobed, then . . .

Leaves arranged opposite each other on the twigs, or do they alternate? If opposite, then . . .

Are leaves heart-shaped or oval? If oval, then . . .

Once you have identified a plant, the plant key can provide a wealth of information about the species, often including its normal geographic range, its general size and shape, and descriptions of fruiting bodies, leaves, and bark. Plant identification is most effective when it is done in a plant's natural setting where you have a wide range of clues to help you.

Identifying Trees

Identifying a tree can be simple. "You can tell a dogwood by its bark," the old-timers say, and they are right. The appearance of bark is one of several important pieces of evidence that can lead to discovering the name of a tree. Other characteristics to notice when identifying trees for a tree inventory are their shape, leaves, and the way they fit into their environment.

Extremely old: A bristlecone pine tree growing at an elevation of 10,000 feet in the White Mountains in California is estimated to be more than 4,500 years old.

Field Botany

Tree Shape

Some trees spread great branches of leaves toward the sky to absorb as much sunlight as possible. Other trees have shorter, tighter shapes that help them endure storms and shed snow. Here are some of the most common tree shapes.

Vase **Pyramid** **Column**

Palm **Weeping** **Round**

Cone **Irregular** **Oval**

PLANT SCIENCE

Field Botany

Peeling

Bark

Tree bark is notable for its variation in shape and texture. Some barks have distinctive features. For instance, the bark of the ponderosa pine smells of vanilla. Some varieties of bark are shown here.

Plated

Smooth

Furrowed

Flaked

Leaves

Leaves are probably the most commonly used clues for determining a tree's identity. For starters, leaves of conifer trees are shaped like needles or scales. Those of deciduous trees are broad, and might appear singly, in various combinations, or in sets that alternate on a branch or are opposite one another. Basic leaf shapes of broad-leaf trees are shown here.

Plant Communities, Habitats, and Niches

A field botanist studies plants from several different perspectives. In nature, plants live in plant communities. A plant community consists of many different plant species living in the same area. Two examples of plant communities are a tallgrass prairie in Kansas that contains grasses and wildflower species, and a plant community in the desert foothills of southern Arizona populated by creosote trees, shrubs, and giant saguaro cacti.

Within the plant community, individual plant species also occupy unique spaces. Just as humans live in specific houses or apartments, plants live in specific spaces. These places where plants live are their habitats. The habitat of a cottonwood tree is along the banks of meandering rivers in the Midwest and western United States. The high mountain slopes of Montana and Colorado are the habitat of whitebark pine trees.

Within any habitat, the food, shelter, and other resources are divided into separate niches. The niche of a plant or animal species is its role in the community. The niche of fungi, for example, is to take nutrients from dead or dying trees and also to release those nutrients back into the environment in a form that other organisms can use.

Narrow **Lobed fan**

Egg-shaped **Heart-shaped**

Veined fan **Long pointed**

Field Botany

Field botanists have developed special methods for studying plant communities. Because it would be impossible to identify the characteristics of every single one of the thousands of plant species in a study area, field botanists conduct plant samplings to estimate what a larger plant community is like. Even though only a few plants are recorded with plant-sampling techniques, this record still gives the field botanist an accurate estimate of what the rest of the plant community is like.

Sampling Plant Communities With Transects

A transect is a continuous line laid out through one or more plant communities. This line is used as a reference point for taking samples of plant characteristics. Transects work best in areas that contain widely spaced plants, such as an open forest. Here's how to set up a transect through a plant community made up of trees.

- Use a string or tape measure to lay out a line at least 500 feet long through an area containing some trees.

- Use a notebook to record the location of the transect, your name, the date, and the weather conditions. Record any information about the nonliving things along the transect, as well as the type of soil.

- Draw a line 5 inches long across the middle of a sheet of paper in your notebook. Make marks on the line at every inch to represent every 100 feet of your transect.

- Starting at one end of the transect, walk slowly toward the other end. Stop whenever you see a tree within 10 feet of the transect line. Mark on your transect graph the location of each tree. Measure the diameter of each tree at a height of 4 feet off the ground, and record this measurement.

- Continue to identify, measure, and record every tree along the transect line.

- When you have finished, you will have mapped a sampling of the trees in the plant community.

- Make a graph or chart using the information you gathered. Show the percentages of tree species present and the tree trunk diameter measurements.

Sampling Plant Communities With Nested Plots

To sample mixed plant communities of trees, shrubs, and grasses, field botanists often use nested plots. In nested-plot sampling, plots of different sizes are used to sample vegetation of different sizes. Large plots are used to sample large trees; medium plots are used to sample smaller trees and shrubs; and the smallest plots are used to sample wildflowers, ferns, and other small plants. The smallest plot is located inside the medium plot, which is located inside the largest plot—hence all plots are nested.

Here's how you can sample a plant community using the nested-plot technique.

Find a plant community that contains a mix of large and small plants, including trees, shrubs, grasses, and flowers.

Step 1—Use a notebook to record the location of the plant community, your name, the date, and the weather conditions. Record any information about the nonliving things. Note the type of soil.

Step 2—Make a diagram in your notebook showing the plots that you lay out.

Step 3—Use a tape measure to mark off a large plot that is 100 by 100 feet square. Identify and map all the large trees that grow in this plot. Record your findings on the diagram in your notebook.

Step 4—Inside of the large plot, make a second smaller plot that is 10 by 10 feet square. Identify and map all medium-size plants (small trees and shrubs) in this plot, and record your findings in your notebook.

Step 5—Inside of the medium plot you made in the previous step, mark off your last (and smallest) plot, 4 by 4 feet square. Identify and map all the small plants in this plot, including grasses and wildflowers.

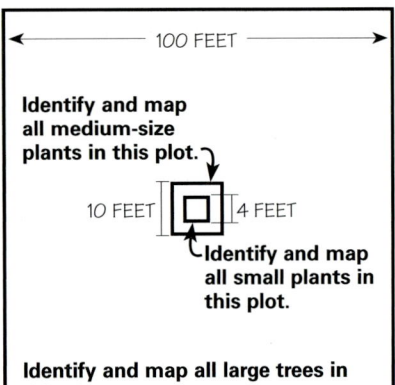

Rare, Threatened, and Endangered Plants

Increasing population growth, cultivation of land for crops, and the growth of cities and suburbs are causing plant habitat losses. As the habitat of a plant is lost, the plant itself may no longer be able to propagate, and the numbers of that plant species may begin to decline. Plants that were once common may become rare or may disappear entirely.

Field botanists help identify habitats of plant species and measure whether plant populations are increasing or decreasing over time. The information gathered by field botanists helps alert land managers and the public that certain plant species may be in danger. This knowledge can then be used to develop land-use policies and to educate the public to help protect the plants.

A plant or animal species that has so few individuals left that it is in danger of dying out is called an endangered species. A threatened species is a plant or animal species that is losing members at such a rate that they will become endangered if nothing is done to change the situation. The federal government has officially classified about 750 threatened or endangered plant species in the United States. Plant scientists believe that more than 30,000 flowering plants, ferns, and trees are threatened or endangered in the world, mostly due to loss of habitat.

= Field Botany

Sample Questions for an Herbarium Visit	Sample Questions for a Conservation Organization Visit
• How do researchers use the plant specimens?	• What are some of the conservation activities the organization carries out?
• Do you have any voucher specimens of plants that are rare in our state?	• What are some threats to rare plants?
• What tools and references do botanists at the herbarium use?	• What land management techniques does the organization use to protect native plants?

Visiting an Herbarium or Plant Conservation Organization

Herbariums are plant specimen libraries, usually housed in universities or botanical gardens. They are a valuable resource for plant scientists and researchers because their collections often include voucher specimens of rare or extinct plants. The specimens are systematically arranged for reference. Some are arranged alphabetically according to botanic classifications (family, genus, and species). Others are arranged geographically.

Because these voucher specimens are intended for long-term study and safekeeping, all mounting supplies and storage materials must be durable and archival (free of acids and other compounds that might cause deterioration or discoloration over time). They must be handled carefully to avoid damaging the fragile specimens. The collections are stored inside dust-proof boxes or cabinets in areas with controlled temperature and humidity.

Plant conservation organizations work to preserve diversity in the plant world. They include private organizations such as the Nature Conservancy and the Center for Plant Conservation, as well as government agencies such as each state's department of natural resources. These organizations are concerned with identifying plant species that may be in danger of dying out and drafting plans to help such plants survive.

To arrange a visit to an herbarium or a plant conservation organization, check your local telephone book or search the Internet (with your parent's permission) to find out if there is one close enough for you to visit. Before you visit, prepare a list of questions. Take a notebook so you can write down your observations and the answers to your questions.

If you cannot visit an herbarium in person, visit the website (with your parent's permission) of one of the herbariums listed in the resources section.

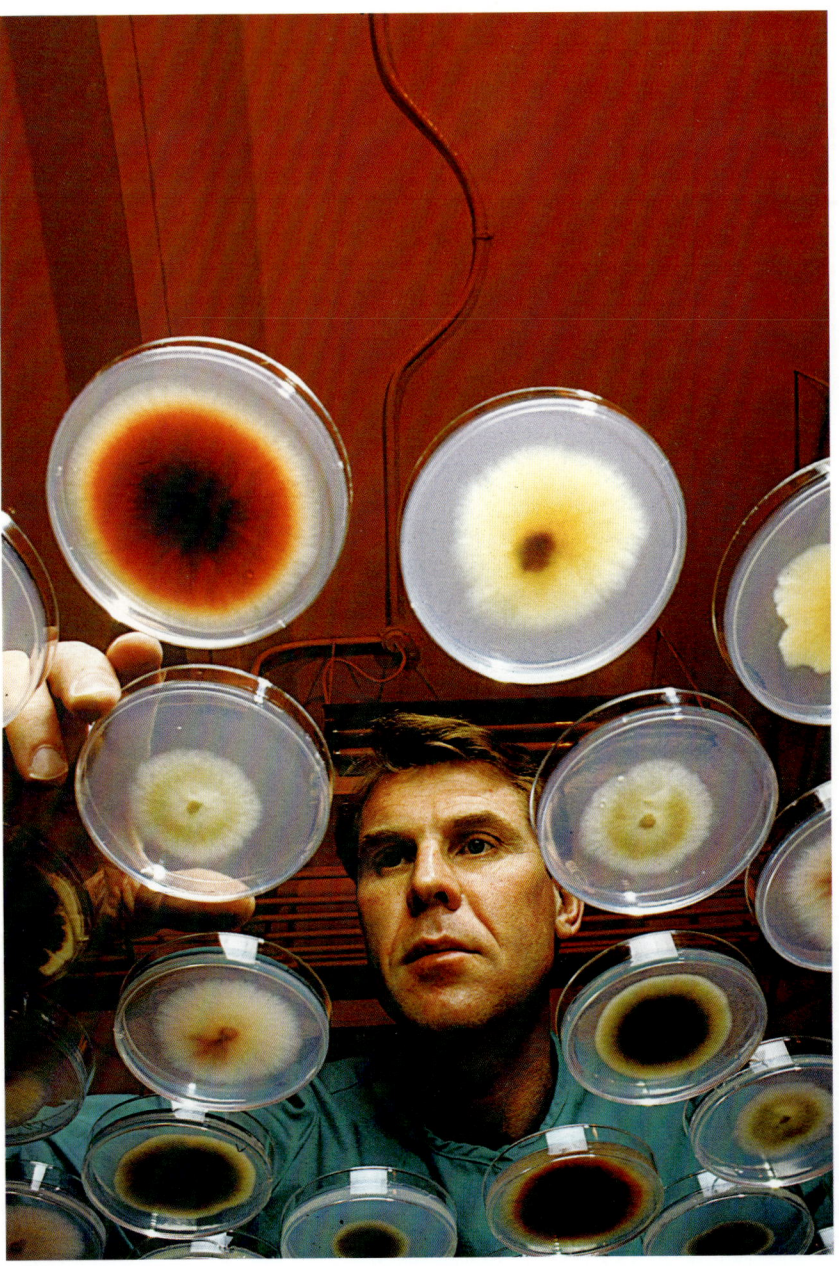

Careers in Plant Science

Pursuing a career in plant science can be very rewarding. If you enjoy being outdoors, then working in field botany or on a farm might interest you. If you have both a green thumb and a flair for design, you might pursue a career as a landscape designer. Would you like helping other people with plant problems? Then perhaps you could become a county extension agent for the federal government, giving advice to community members.

Plant Science Careers You Might Choose

Agronomists help develop better and safer ways to produce the food and plant materials that are essential to society. Agronomists include laboratory researchers who study how to produce safer pesticides and fertilizers. Other agronomists study the genetic composition of plants and design methods to improve plant characteristics. Agronomists who do research with a government laboratory or corporation usually have a master's or doctorate degree.

A farmer could be considered an agronomist. To be a good farmer in today's world, you need to be a good plant scientist. Growing crops requires knowledge of botany, chemistry, soil science, and business management. On-farm experience is one of the best ways to learn what is required if you want to pursue a career in farming. If you do not live on a farm, you can still gain valuable exposure to farm life through vocational agriculture courses in high school, 4-H clubs, the National FFA Organization (formerly Future Farmers of America), or by volunteering to work on a farm. Many farmers today have an associate or bachelor's degree in some field of agriculture or biology.

About 40 percent of all plant scientists in the United States work for some government agency, either as county extension agents, state agricultural department employees, USDA researchers, or other positions.

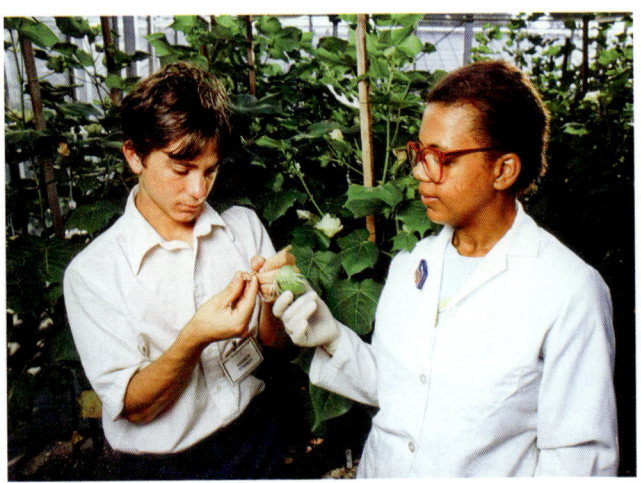

Horticulturists study the science and art of growing flowers, fruits, plants, and vegetables. Horticulturists often have college degrees in landscape design, horticulture, or business management. Horticulturists may work in greenhouses or with farm agencies as producers, marketers, or inspectors. They might also do landscape design at a zoo or park. They can recommend the type of plants and flowers that would thrive in a particular climate and soil as well as offer advice on how to treat unhealthy plants.

Field botanists include plant ecologists, who study how plants are influenced by climate, soils, other plants, and animals, including man. Field botanists are often hired by state and federal agencies to conduct inventories of rare and endangered plant species. Private organizations and universities also employ field botanists to help them understand why plants grow in certain areas and to discover new plant species that might be used in new medicines and foods.

You will need at least a bachelor's degree in botany or plant ecology to be a field botanist. Most field botanists continue their education, earning a master's degree or doctorate. Field botanists need to enjoy working outdoors, and must develop observation skills. Many field botanists spend their summers working in natural areas, observing and recording information about plant species and plant communities.

Plant Science Resources

Scouting Literature

Fieldbook; Boy Scout Journal; Environmental Science, Gardening, Landscape Architecture, Soil and Water Conservation, Insect Study, Forestry, and *Nature* merit badge pamphlets

> Visit the Boy Scouts of America's official retail website (with your parent's permission) at http://www.scoutstuff.org for a complete listing of all merit badge pamphlets and other helpful Scouting materials and supplies.

Books

Bartholomew, Mel. *All New Square Foot Gardening*. Cool Springs Press, 2006.

Bryant, Geoff. *Plant Propagation A to Z: Growing Plants for Free*. Firefly Books Ltd. 2006.

Elzer-Peters, Katie. *Beginner's Illustrated Guide to Gardening: Techniques to Help You Get Started*. Cool Springs Press, 2012.

Jeavons, John. *How to Grow More Vegetables*, 8th ed. Ten Speed Press, 2012.

Kujawski, Jennifer. *The Week-by-Week Vegetable Gardener's Handbook: Make the Most of Your Growing Season*. Storey Publishing, 2011.

Madigan, Carleen. *The Backyard Homestead: Produce All the Food You Need on Just a Quarter Acre!* Story Publishing, 2009.

Pleasant, Barbara. *Starter Vegetable Gardens: 24 No-Fail Plans for Small Organic Gardens*. Storey Publishing, 2010.

Organizations and Websites

American Association of Botanical Gardens and Arboreta
Telephone: 302-655-7100

American Horticultural Society
Website: http://www.ahs.org

ATTRA—National Sustainable Agriculture Information Service
Toll-free telephone: 800-346-9140
Website: http://www.attra.ncat.org

Botanical Society of America
Telephone: 314-577-9566
Website: http://www.botany.org

Botanique: Portal to Gardens, Arboreta, and Nature Sites
Website: http://www.botanique.com/tourmast.html

PLANT SCIENCE RESOURCES

Center for Plant Conservation
Telephone: 314-577-9450
Website: http://www.centerforplantconservation.org

Endangered Species Program
U.S. Fish and Wildlife Service
Website: http://www.fws.gov/endangered

National FFA Organization
Telephone: 317-802-6060
Website: http://www.ffa.org

InvasiveSpecies.org
Website: http://www.invasive.org

Native Plant Information Network
Telephone: 512-292-4200
Website: http://www.wildflower.org

The Nature Conservancy
Telephone: 703-841-5300
Website: http://www.nature.org

University of Florida Herbarium
Telephone: 352-392-1721 ext. 212
Website: http://www.flmnh.ufl.edu/herbarium

USDA Cooperative Extension System Office Locator Map
Website: http://www.csrees.usda.gov/Extension

U.S. National Arboretum
Telephone: 202-245-2726
Website: http://www.usna.usda.gov

USDA National Agricultural Statistics Service
Toll-free telephone: 800-727-9540
Website: http://www.nass.usda.gov

USDA Plants Database
Website: http://plants.usda.gov

Acknowledgments

For his help in writing this edition of the *Plant Science* merit badge pamphlet, the Boy Scouts of America thanks Eagle Scout Jeff Birkby, former camp ranger and conservationist at Philmont Scout Ranch.

The Boy Scouts of America is grateful to the men and women serving on the Merit Badge Maintenance Task Force for the improvements made in updating this pamphlet.

Photo and Illustration Credits

Lynn Betts, U.S. Department of Agriculture, Natural Resources Conservation Service, courtesy—page 54

John D. Byrd, Mississippi State University, Bugwood.org, courtesy—page 46 (*center*)

Bill Cook, Michigan State University, Forestryimages.org, courtesy—page 84 (*bottom left*)

Steve Dewey, Utah State University, Bugwood.org, courtesy—page 46 (*bottom*)

Division of Plant Industry Archive, Florida Department of Agriculture and Consumer Services, Bugwood.org, courtesy—page 45 (*center*)

Chris Evans, River to River CWMA, Bugwood.org, courtesy—page 46 (*top*)

HAAP Media Ltd., courtesy—cover (*grasshopper, ladybird beetle*)

Linda Haugen, USDA Forest Service, Bugwood.org, courtesy—page 30

Plant Science Resources

©Jupiterimages.com—pages 14, 23, and 51–52

George Markham, USA Forest Service, Bugwood.org, courtesy—page 49 (*center*)

Paul A. Mistrella, USDA Forest Service, Bugwood.org, courtesy—page 44

National Renewable Energy Laboratory/Warren Gretz, courtesy—page 34

©Photos.com—cover (*corn, young plants, wildflowers*); pages 17 (*center and bottom*), 21, 50, 84 (*top and both center*), and 85 (*all*)

Dave Powell, USDA Forest Service, Bugwood.org, courtesy—pages 48 (*top*) and 49 (*top*)

©Realworld Imagery Inc.—page 83 (*all*)

R. J. Reynolds Tobacco Company Slide Set, R. J. Reynolds Tobacco Co., Bugwood.org, courtesy—page 43 (*top*)

Jan Samanek, State Phytosanitary Administration, Bugwood.org, courtesy—page 48 (*bottom*)

Shutterstock.com—page 19 (photomatz/Shutterstock.com, courtesy)

David Stephens, Bugwood.org, courtesy—page 15 (*bottom*)

Jim Story, Montana State University, Bugwood.org, courtesy—page 47 (*bottom*)

Dan Tenaglia, Missouriplants.com, Bugwood.org, courtesy—page 47 (*top*)

Barbara Tokarska-Guzik, University of Silesia, Bugwood.org, courtesy—page 47 (*center*)

University of Georgia Archive, University of Georgia, Bugwood.org, courtesy—page 43 (*bottom*)

University of Michigan Herbarium, courtesy—page 18

U.S. Department of Agriculture, courtesy—page 43 (*center*)

USDA Agricultural Resource Service, courtesy—pages 37 (*top*), 45 (*top*), and 84 (*bottom right*)

USDA Agricultural Resource Service/Scott Bauer, courtesy—pages 32, 33 (*top*), 36, 56, 90, and 92

USDA Agricultural Resource Service/Bruce Fritz, courtesy—page 53

USDA Agricultural Resource Service/Yue Jin, courtesy—page 45 (*bottom*)

USDA Agricultural Resource Service/David Nance, courtesy—page 24

USDA Agricultural Resource Service/Poisonous Research Laboratory, courtesy—page 17 (*top*)

USDA Agricultural Resource Service/Keith Weller, courtesy—pages 37 (*bottom*) and 42

U.S. Department of Agriculture/Charles Herron, courtesy—page 33 (*bottom*)

U.S. Department of Agriculture/Bob Nichols, courtesy—page 93

Theodore Webster, USDA Agricultural Resource Service, Bugwood.org, courtesy—page 49 (*bottom*)

All other photos and illustrations not mentioned above are the property of or are protected by the Boy Scouts of America.

Daniel Giles—pages 12, 28 (*center, bottom*), 39–40 (*all*), 65 (*photo*), 69–70 (*all*), 75, 78, and 86

John McDearmon—all illustrations on pages 16, 24–25, 27, 29, 64–65, 68, 72, and 81